MOCHI'S WAR

MOCHI'S WAR

The Tragedy of Sand Creek

Chris Enss and Howard Kazanjian

TWODOT®

GUILFORD, CONNECTICUT
HELENA, MONTANA

A · TWODOT® · BOOK
An imprint of Rowman & Littlefield
Distributed by NATIONAL BOOK NETWORK

British Library Cataloguing in Publication Information Available

Library of Congress Cataloging-in-Publication Data
Enss, Chris, 1961-
Mochi's war : the tragedy of Sand Creek / Chris Enss and Howard Kazanjian. — 1st edition.
pages cm
Includes bibliographical references and index.
ISBN 978-0-7627-6077-0 (pbk. : alk. paper) — ISBN 978-1-4930-1394-4 (e-book : alk. paper)
1. Mochi, approximately 1841-1881. 2. Sand Creek Massacre, Colo., 1864. 3. Cheyenne Indians—
Biography. 4. Cheyenne Indians—Wars, 1864. 5. Indian prisoners—Florida—Castillo de San Marcos
National Monument (Saint Augustine)—Biography. 6. Prisoners of war—Florida—Castillo de San
Marcos National Monument (Saint Augustine)—Biography. 7. Indians of North America—Reloca-
tion—Florida—Castillo de San Marcos National Monument (Saint Augustine) 8. Sand Creek Massacre National Historic Site (Colo.) I. Kazanjian, Howard. II. Title. III. Title: Tragedy of Sand Creek.
E83.863.E58 2015
978.8004'97353092—dc23
[B]
2015005372

∞ ™ The paper used in this publication meets the minimum requirements of American National Standard for Information Sciences Permanence of Paper for Printed Library Materials, ANSI/NISO Z39.48-1992.

CONTENTS

ACKNOWLEDGMENTS

This book is intended to be a tribute to those who lost their lives at Sand Creek and those who endured after the tragedy. Half of the royalties from the sale of this book will go to support the Sand Creek National Historic Site.

The following individuals and organizations helped make this work possible: Sara Keckeisen at the Kansas State Historical Society; Tom Mooney at the Nebraska State Historical Society; Sarah Gilmor at the History Colorado Center; Allen Arnold, information technology specialist at Castillo de San Marcos at St. Augustine, Florida; and the Denver Public Library. Alexa Roberts and Eric Sainio at the Sand Creek National Historic Site were kind and generous and we're grateful for their assistance. Special thanks to the talented people at Globe Pequot who skillfully transformed the raw material of this manuscript into a product we're proud to share. We appreciate Erin Turner and her willingness to review a proposal on the subject of Mochi and the Sand Creek Massacre. Erin has been a constant source of encouragement and we are indebted to her.

FOREWORD

Mochi's War encapsulates the story of a ruthless woman warrior who was born out of the pits of the Sand Creek Massacre. The word "warrior" sends a tingle of fear down the spine and conjures up a fierce, merciless fighter seemingly invulnerable to fear or intimidation.

There are many reasons that a Native Indian woman would fight and become one of the warriors. Most nineteenth-century women who fought in battles and conflicts did not pursue the life of a warrior on a permanent basis. Most women fought because there was an urgent need for them to do so, which the reader will find out quickly was the case for this twenty-four-year-old Cheyenne warrior.

Howard Kazanjian and Chris Enss write of the malice in the young woman's heart and the revenge that sat heavily on the edge of her toma-hawk. This woman warrior was willing to fight to the death using blood-thirsty tactics to achieve victory. Hers is not the usual image that we would associate with women, but there were many female Native American warriors.

When asked to name some famous Indian women, most people have difficulty recalling anyone other than Pocahontas or Sacagawea; readers will have no difficulty remembering Mochi, the Cheyenne Warrior, after engaging themselves in *Mochi's War*.

Rebecka Lyman
Cheyenne and Arapaho Tribal Tribune

INTRODUCTION

Mochi was so distinguished for fiend-like fierceness and atrocity that it
was not deemed safe to leave her on the plains. She was a fine looking
Indian woman but as mean as they come.
—*Observation made by a military officer after Mochi's arrest on
March 5, 1875*

Somewhere amid the high plains sage country, the Big Sandy Creek
once ran red with the blood of dozens of Cheyenne and Arapaho men,
women, and children. On November 29, 1864, hundreds of members of
the Colorado Volunteers poured down upon a sleeping Indian camp, leaving in their wake the slaughtered remains of Native Americans who were
scalped and mutilated.[1]

The unprovoked attack on the Indian settlement was led by Colonel
John Milton Chivington, who is said to have ordered every Indian at the
scene killed. To those settlers and traders who had been terrorized by the
Indians and because of exaggerated reports of Indian attacks on families
and troops, the Sand Creek Massacre was regarded by some as proper
retribution on the Indians, and Chivington was revered for his actions.

The event that forced frontiersmen and women to address the serious
issues that had been building between them and the Indians occurred on
June 11, 1864. Rancher Nathan Ward Hungate, his wife, Ellen, and their
two little girls were slaughtered by Indians. Their mutilated bodies were
brought to Denver and put on display in the center of town. The people
there were thrown into a panic. In the following weeks, at the mere
mention of Indians in the outlying areas, women and children were sent to

homes that were fortified and guarded. Plains travel slowed to a trickle. The supply of kerosene was exhausted, and the settlers had to use candles. [2]

A regiment of one hundred day volunteers known as the Third Colorado Cavalry was organized, and George L. Shoup, a scout during the Civil War, was named the outfit's colonel. At the same time, John Evans, governor of the Colorado Territory, issued a proclamation stating: "Friendly Arapahoe and Cheyenne belonging to the Arkansas River will go to Major Colley, U.S. Indian Agent at Fort Lyon, who will give them a place of safety. . . . The war on hostile Indians will be continued until they are effectually subdued." [3]

On August 29, 1864, before the regiment saw active service, a letter from Cheyenne leader Black Kettle explaining that the Indians had agreed to make peace was delivered to officers at Fort Lyon, 150 miles away from Denver. The letter noted that Cheyenne and Arapaho war parties had prisoners they would like to exchange for Indians being held by the volunteers. [4]

Major E. W. Wynkoop of the First Colorado at Fort Lyon marched his troops to Black Kettle's camp to collect the captives. While there, Wynkoop persuaded the chief to send a delegation to Denver to talk about the conditions for peace.

From Fort Leavenworth, Major General Samuel Ryan Curtis, commander of the Department of Kansas, telegraphed Chivington prior to the conference with the chiefs: "I shall require the bad Indians delivered up; restoration of equal numbers of stock; also hostages to secure. I want no peace till the Indians suffer more." Chivington took the order to heart. [5]

Not everyone agreed that Chivington deserved the praise he received from some after the massacre at Sand Creek. Many politicians and military leaders objected to his savage assault on the village. According to Oklahoma Governor Henry S. Johnson, Chivington's act "brings a revolt in the heart of every American citizen and will stand in history to condemn the civilized government that sought to deal with the question of what to do with the Indian." [6]

The number reportedly killed at Sand Creek varies widely from 63 people to 200. Most historians agree that the death toll was around 160.

0.1. This photo of the Southern Plains delegation was taken in the White House Conservatory on March
reter William Simpson Smith and the Agent S. G. Colley are standing at the left of the group; the white wo
ng at the far right is often identified as Mary Todd Lincoln. The Indians in the front row, left to right: War B
ing in the Water, and Lean Bear of the Cheyenne, and Yellow Wolf of the Kiowas. The identities of the seco
wn. Within eighteen months from the date of this sitting, all four men in the front row were dead. Yellow V
nonia a few days after the picture was taken; War Bonnet and Standing in the Water died in the Sand Cree
y of Congress, LC-DIG-ppmsca-19914

Adding to the tragedy, Black Kettle, a prominent Cheyenne leader, believed he had entered into a peace agreement with the United States Army. Historians say that when the first shots were fired on the camp, Black Kettle raised an American flag and a white cloth of truce to signal the desire to talk peace.

A warrior was born out of the tragedy at Sand Creek—one that would live only to see her slain family avenged. The Cheyenne Indian woman driven to violent and desperate measures was named Mochi. For more than ten years, she engaged in raiding and warfare against the United States government along with her husband, Medicine Water. These Cheyenne renegades became two of the most feared Indians in the American West.

"The Cheyenne hated a liar as a devil hates Holy water," Indian agent Captain Percival G. Lowe wrote in his memoirs in 1896 about the uprising of Mochi and the other outraged Indians who survived the Sand Creek Massacre. "And that is why when they came to know him they hated the white man. They did not crave stealthy murder but wanted their enemies to die an overt and brutal death over what happened on the Sand Creek."[7]

Chivington never anticipated the backlash that occurred. He believed the Sand Creek Massacre would put a stop to the Indians' attacks on wagon train parties and military caravans, but instead it stirred the Plains Indians, specifically the Southern Cheyenne, Kiowa, and Arapaho, into war with systematic attacks on the South Platte Valley from south and southeast and from north and northwest. Fourteen major battles would be fought, from the attack on the Julesburg, Colorado, outpost to the Lone Tree Massacre in Kansas.

The Indian Wars in the West were fought because white trappers, miners, and settlers were invading Indian hunting grounds and ancestral burying spots. They were wars of conquest for the whites and attempts to repulse the invaders by Indians. Beginning with the first Sioux War in 1854 and culminating in the last grand stand of the Indians in 1876, the government, and occasionally the Indians, broke treaties between each other over and over again.

The events at Sand Creek motivated Mochi to embark on a decade-long reign of terror. With each raid she remembered the horror of the massacre, and it goaded her on to commit brutal outrages on those encroaching on Indian soil. The war between the Indians and the government lasted ten years after the Sand Creek Massacre occurred. Mochi's war ended with her arrest and imprisonment in 1875.

Chivington's name was disgraced by Sand Creek. He had been a well-known minister and hero of the Civil War battle of Glorietta Pass, New Mexico. Even before his death in July 1891 his name had become synonymous with murder and controversy. Mochi's name as well brought to mind brutality and killing. She didn't start the battle that resulted in her family's demise, but she did contribute to the terror that swept across the plains from 1865 to 1874.

I

TRAGEDY AT LITTLE BLUE RIVER

In the spring of 1875, a locomotive pulling several freight cars left Fort Leavenworth, Kansas, bound for Fort Marion, Florida. Thirty-three Cheyenne Indian prisoners were on board; only one was a woman. Her name was Mochi, which means Buffalo Calf Woman. She made the trip shackled and chained to her husband, a warrior named Medicine Water. The irons affixed to the thirty-four-year-old woman's wrists and ankles were so tight they cut into her skin and made them bleed. Her flesh would be permanently scarred by the time the six-week journey to Florida came to an end.[1]

Hundreds of curious men, women, and children witnessed the Indian captives being taken away. Some of the onlookers shouted at the prisoners and called them "murderers" and "savages." Neither Mochi nor the other Indians responded. They didn't consider killing the settlers during their raids on homesteads in Nebraska and Kansas as criminal. Driven by the desire to stop pioneers from taking over their homeland and by revenge for the Cheyenne and Arapaho Indians slaughtered by the invading force, Mochi went to war. She would suffer the consequence.[2]

The prison that would be Mochi's home for more than two years was the oldest fortification on the continent. It covered an acre of ground and accommodated a garrison of 1,000 men. Building of the fort began in 1620 and was completed in 1856. A Spanish coat of arms and the name of the chief engineer of the structure, along with the date the fort was completed, were carved into the stone above the entrance.[3]

Cheyenne Indians were relegated to the north side of Fort Marion along with Arapaho inmates. The Comanche, Kiowa, and Caddo shared the west side. Mochi and Medicine Water were assigned to an area away from the rest of the Cheyenne captives because they were considered too dangerous to be with the other Indians.[4] Mochi was the only Native American woman to be incarcerated by the United States Army as a prisoner of war. There were other female residents at the fort, but they were wives of the prisoners who didn't want to be without their husbands.[5]

Mochi contemplated escaping when she first arrived, but the fort walls were sixteen feet thick and thirty feet high in spots. She slowly surrendered her physical self to the sentence she had been given, but her mind and heart could not be contained. The tragic circumstances that led to imprisonment in Florida haunted her. For Mochi, hardship and heartache began at a place in Colorado called Sand Creek.[6]

Mochi was born in 1841 in Yellowstone, Wyoming. Her parents, whose names have been lost with time, adored their daughter. According to Cheyenne Indian historian Ann Strange Owl-Raben, Mochi's childhood was not unlike that of any other Cheyenne. As was the custom, paternal elders named Mochi and blessed her life at a traditional naming ceremony. At the age of nine Mochi began learning how to skin and tan the hides of the animals hunted for the tribe. She was also taught how to sew, bead, identify herbs, and manage a lodge, along with a number of other tasks specific to Cheyenne girls.[7]

By the time Mochi was a teenager, she was well acquainted with all the tasks for which Cheyenne women were responsible. In addition to cooking and cleaning, women built their family's lodge and dragged the heavy posts used to make the tepee whenever the tribe moved. Cheyenne women took part in administering traditional medicines, storytelling, creating artwork, and playing music.[8]

1.1. **Exterior of Fort Marion in Saint Augustine, Florida, State Archives of Florida, *Florida Memory***

Mochi married her first husband when she was in her early teens. As custom dictated, she was carried into the wedding lodge by her new husband's best friend. "She was dressed in clothing her husband had brought her, and his other gifts covered her arms and legs," Ann Strange Owl-Raban noted about Mochi in her book *Four Great Rivers to Cross*. Mochi also wore a protective rope around her waist under her clothes. The rope wound around her thighs and extended to her knees. This rope was worn for the first few nights of a marriage so the newlyweds could get to know one another well without relying solely on the physical aspect of a relationship. "The rope was to be respected by the groom as long as the bride decided to wear it," Owl-Raban noted about the Cheyenne marriage ceremony.[9]

Chastity was highly respected by Cheyenne men and women. Great respect was given to men and women who did not consummate their marriage until months after their marriage ceremony. Consequently, women placed a high value on chastity as an expression of sacrifice and renewing. Cheyenne law notes that "the woman is above everything because the creator has given her power to spread people to cover the face of the earth."[10]

Mochi and her husband lived among their people with no other hope than that possessed by their ancestors, to live happily raising children of their own on the land that had been occupied for centuries by the Cheyenne Indians.

Sixteen-year-old Laura Louise Roper hoped for roughly the same in life as Mochi. Born in Pennsylvania on June 16, 1848, to Hon. Joseph and Sophia Roper, Laura was considered by friends and neighbors to be a beautiful girl.[11] In early 1864, she accepted the proposal of a young wagon train driver named Marshall B. Kelley, and the couple planned to build a homestead along the Little Blue River in southern Nebraska. Marshall had already established a settlement several miles from a military outpost near what is now the town of Oak, Nebraska. Once they were married, Laura and Marshall were going to live in a log house and farm. On August 7, 1864, a band of Cheyenne Indians attacked the pioneers in and around the settlement. Among those assaulted was Laura Roper.[12]

An article in the December 2, 1926, edition of the *Marysville Advocate-Democrat* newspaper reported that the great "western migration of settlers prompted the Little Blue River tragedy as well as many others like it." Indians could see that with the increase in white sojourners the buffalo would either be exterminated or driven away and the red man would be left without food. "The total population of the Plains tribes was around 60,000," the newspaper noted. "The coming of the white man drove the Indians to inaugurate defensive measures to save their ancient home and hunting grounds. And it so appears that the Kiowa, Apache, Cheyenne, with the Brule, Oglala, and Missouri Sioux agreed to drive the white man out of their domain by any means that they could devise."[13]

Laura and her family had experienced difficulties with the Indians prior to August 7, 1864. In late June several of Joseph Roper's horses had been stolen, along with supplies from his ranch house. "My father told me as I left to visit neighbors the day tragedy struck—not to come home alone as the Indians might be lurking around," Laura explained to a reporter at the *Beatrice Daily Sun* in January 1927.[14] Her father was right. At four o'clock in the afternoon, Laura was on her way back from visiting with neighbors when a band of Cheyenne warriors overtook her and the friends with her. "Mr. Eubanks, his wife and two children and myself started for my home which was about a mile and a half away," an article in the November 5, 1884, edition of the *Logansport Journal* noted.[15] Laura continued:

> At the same time Mr. Eubanks's father and his little nephew nine years of age started the opposite direction. Before they reached their destination the Indians killed the old man and took the boy prisoner and also killed their team.
>
> We had gotten about one-half mile when we came to a place in the road which would round the bluff and was called "The Narrows" because the road was so narrow at the place. Mr. Eubanks was barefooted and got a sliver in his foot and said he would stop and get it out and for us to walk on, and he would overtake us. We had gone about fifty yards around the bluff when we stopped to wait for him. Just then we heard terrible yells. I said I thought it was Indians. So we turned and ran back until we came in sight of Mr. Eubanks and he was running toward the house. We could not see the Indians at the house and they were chasing Mr. Eubanks's sister—a girl of about seventeen years old. Then Mr. Eubanks turned and ran toward the river. And just as he got to the edge of the sand bar the Indians shot and killed him. His two brothers that were in the house started to run up a draw and they were both killed. The sister started to run toward us and they tried to take her prisoner and she fought them and they stabbed her and killed her.

Figure 1.2.   Plains Indian captives of the Little Blue River Raid. Laura Roper is in the center holding Isabel[
with Ambrose Asher on her left, and Danny Marble on her right. The four were released to the Army on S
1864. Nebraska State Historical Society

By this time we had gotten into the timber. I was carrying Mr. Eubanks's little girl about four years old and Mrs. Eubanks had her baby boy who was six months old. We ran right into a buffalo wallow and sat down at the edge of the wallow. By this time the Indians had killed everyone at the house and started for my father's place. They raced their horses and came right at us. I had taken off my slippers and was carrying them in my hand. They charged at me and knocked me down and draped a chain around my neck several times. Then they took us all by the hand and told us to come and picked us up and put us on the horses and took us back to Mr. Eubanks's house.

On the way back we saw this girl—Mr. Eubanks's sister lying beside a path about one hundred yards from the house. We could see where they had stabbed her but she was not quite dead then. We saw her throw her arm over her head. We then went on to the house. We had not been there but a few minutes when an Indian rode up with this girl's scalp on a spear. We knew it was hers because it was still dripping with blood. He was yelling like a mad man.

When they got to the house they got us off the horses and began destroying everything in the house. They broke the stove, dishes, guns, and emptied the feather beds. They were there about an hour. While we were there they let us wander around and didn't seem to pay much attention to us. In the meantime we went over to a little draw close to the house and I took my chain off my neck. Mrs. Eubanks got the baby two dresses while we were there, also a sunbonnet for herself. By that time it was about six o'clock. Then they put us on the horses behind them and started south and my father lived west.

We crossed the Little Blue River and still went south. Traveled all night. About the middle of the night an Indian rode up behind me and asked me if I was afraid the Indians would kill me. I said: "No. I wasn't, because I thought if they intended killing me they would have done so at the start." He said, "No, I don't think they will kill you. I don't think they will keep you long before they will give you up."

We rode all next day. There were just seven Indians that had captured us but that afternoon about five more joined us and then I got a horse by myself. The second night we went down a deep ditch and my saddle came off and the pony in trying to get up hit me with his hoof and broke my nose. The Indians had taken a sheet they had gotten at Mrs. Eubanks's and wiped the blood from my face, and nearly whipped the pony to death. Then the Indian that captured me took me on the horse with him and we rode the rest of the night and the next day until about two o'clock. In the meantime we only had dried buffalo meat to eat. Eventually they killed a turkey and fed us. By this time my face had swollen until I could scarcely see. They unsaddled their horses and motioned for us to lie and rest. Here they painted my face with red paint and by the morning the swelling had gone down.

They separated Mrs. Eubanks from her daughter and she screamed and cried the whole time. When we got ready to leave the Indian that captured the little girl wanted to take her on his horse with him and of course she screamed and wanted to go to her mother. The Indian grabbed her by her hair and he drew out his hunting knife and I thought he was going to kill her. I ran and grabbed the knife and he just laughed. [16]

Laura, Mrs. Eubanks, and the two children were taken to the Indians' camp and delivered to the squaws. The four were held hostage at the camp for two months. Because Laura had stopped the Indians from scalping the Eubanks's child, the Indians assumed that Mrs. Eubanks's daughter belonged to her. During the time Laura was with the Indians she learned they were Cheyenne and Arapaho Indians and that the Cheyenne chief was Black Kettle and the Arapaho chief was Left Hand. [17]

Lucinda Eubanks's account of her captivity among the Indians was as frightening as Laura Roper's. According to a statement Mrs. Eubanks made to army officers on June 22, 1865, even before she had been kidnapped in August of 1864 (along with her children and nephew), her home had been robbed and burned. [18] Mrs. Eubanks reported:

When first taken by the Cheyenne, I was taken to the lodge of an old chief whose name I do not recollect. He forced me, by the most terrible threats and menaces, to yield my person to him. He treated me as his wife. He traded me to Two Face, a Sioux, who did not treat me as a wife, but forced me to do all menial labor done by squaws, and he beat me terribly.

Two Face traded me to Black Foot who treated me as his wife, and because I resisted him his squaws abused and ill-used me. Black Foot also beat me unmercifully, and the Indians generally treated me as though I was a dog, on account of my showing so much detestation toward Black Foot. Black Foot traded me again. I then received better treatment. I was better treated among the Sioux than the Cheyenne, that is, the Sioux gave me more to eat. When with the Cheyenne, I was often hungry.

My purchase from the Cheyenne was made early last fall and I remained with the Sioux until May 1865. During the winter the Cheyenne came to buy me and my son for the purpose of burning us, but Two Face would not let them have me. During the winter we were on the North Platte, the Indians were killing the whites all the time and running off their stock. They would bring in the scalps of the whites and show them to me and laugh about it. They ordered me frequently to wean my baby, but I always refused for I felt convinced if he was weaned they would take him from me and I should never see him again. [19]

News of the tragedy at the Little Blue River horrified pioneers, and warfare between the Indians and the whites escalated. In 1864, Major General G. M. Dodge, who was in charge of all the military forces in the west, wrote to Washington: "I desire that the government may understand that it has either got to abandon the country west entirely to the Indians or meet the war issue presented; there are 25,000 warriors in open hostilities, and never before have we had so extensive a war on the plains and an enemy so well supplied as now." [20]

However savage the treatment of white settlers, Mochi and other Cheyenne Indians believed the action was justified. According to the treaty between the United States and the Cheyenne and Arapaho Indians drafted in February 1860, the Indians were persuaded to sell the government their land twelve miles below Fort Wise, Colorado, at the mouth of the Big Sandy, running to the Arkansas River one hundred miles to within five miles of the mouth of the Huerfano River. In exchange, the two Nations were to maintain an area of their native land one hundred miles long and fifteen miles wide, and no whites would be allowed to settle there. [21]

"This treaty has been in contemplation by our Government for a number of years," an article in the March 23, 1861, edition of the *Indiana State Guard* noted about the agreement between the United States and the Indians. "The purchase and treaty secured to our Government Pike's Peak and all the gold fields of the region." [22]

Westward pioneers were not satisfied to hold to the area allocated to the United States, and it proved too hard for the few government officials available to patrol the boundaries. White settlers encroached on Indian land and threatened the Native Americans' way of life. They killed and drove off the buffalo the Indians used to survive. The Indians left the area where they agreed to stay in order to hunt. Peace did not last, and both conventional and guerrilla warfare broke out between the Indians and the United States military.[23]

The Dog Soldiers, a band of Cheyenne Indian warriors who refused to submit to any treaty, became a force to reckon with for United States troops on the plains. The Dog Soldiers raided settlements in revenge for the white men pushing their way onto Indian land.[24] Among the Dog Soldiers that distinguished themselves were warriors such as Roman Nose, Dull Knife, Tangle Hair, and eventually Mochi.[25]

The raid on the Little Blue River reached an end for Laura Roper in mid-September 1864, when she was turned over to the United States Cavalry. Laura was taken by the troops to Denver, where she remained until a wagon train could transport her back to Nebraska. Mrs. Eubanks and her son were with the Indians for more than a year before she escaped.[26] What happened to Mrs. Eubanks' little girl remains a mystery. Initially thought to be Laura's daughter, the child was eventually taken from Laura. She speculated that the child was likely killed and buried in an unmarked grave.

According to the March 20, 1907, edition of the *Beatrice Daily Sun*, Dog Soldier Two Face and two of his men escorted the captive to Fort Laramie, Wyoming. A deal had been struck with the Cheyenne to surrender Laura in return for ponies, blankets, and sugar. "But when it was found how cruelly she and the others had been treated the armistice was violated and the three Indians were arrested and hanged in chains on a bluff north of the fort," the *Beatrice Daily Sun* noted. "The bodies of Two Face and his men remained there until the crows picked the flesh from their bones," the article concluded.[27]

Black Kettle, one of the Cheyenne Indians' most respected leaders, recognized there would be further retaliation against the Indians if a peace agreement was not reached.[28] John Evans, governor of the territory of Colorado, was disinclined to make peace. In addition to the blood raids made on white settlers, the Cheyenne had disrupted mail services and stage travel and prevented food and other provisions from reaching military outposts. Governor Evans sought permission from the federal government to organize a volunteer cavalry regiment to deal with Indians who refused to conform. The Third Colorado Cavalry was born.[29] Later known as the "Bloodless Third," the regiment was commanded by Colonel George L. Shoup and assigned to the Colorado district commanded by Governor Evans's dear friend, Colonel John M. Chivington.[30]

Regardless of the influx of troops to the area, Black Kettle believed that peace was still a possibility and trusted that the government would ultimately honor the Fort Wise treaty, which granted Indians protection on designated land. The Cheyenne left the Little Blue Valley and went west. Black Kettle and the other Indians settled in an area called Sand Creek.[31]

According to the memoirs of George Bent, a Cheyenne Indian who was an interpreter for the government and who later chose to fight as a Cheyenne warrior, "Sand Creek heads in the ridge country to the southeast of Denver and flows in a great half-circle toward the east and then toward the south, entering the Arkansas River some miles below Fort Lyon and near the west line of Kansas."[32] The Cheyenne referred to the spot as "Poeneo o'hee" or Dry Creek. The Indian village consisted of 130 lodges scattered irregularly for about a mile along the northern bank of the dry creek bed. A team of five to six hundred ponies were on one side of the Cheyenne Indian camp with a smaller team on the opposite side.[33]

In September 1864, less than a year prior to the Cheyenne moving to Sand Creek, Black Kettle had visited Washington, D.C., and met with Abraham Lincoln to discuss the trials the Cheyenne Indians faced at the hand of the United States government. At that time politicians assured Black Kettle that they had every intention of protecting friendly Indians who remained on the triangular section of territory bound by the Sand Creek and Arkansas rivers.[34]

During Black Kettle's time at the Capitol, the president gave him medals to wear, and Colonel A. B. Greenwood, the commissioner of Indian affairs, presented Black Kettle with a large United States flag.[35] Colonel Greenwood told the Indian chief that as long as the flag flew above him no soldier would ever fire upon him. According to the September 15, 1917, edition of the *North Hill Record*, "Black Kettle was very proud of his flag and when in permanent camp always mounted it to a pole above his tepee. It was flying over his tepee at Sand Creek."[36]

The U.S. flag was flying over Fort Marion the day Mochi was deposited at the Florida prison, too.[37] It fluttered from the staff in the breezy, warm weather in much the same way Black Kettle's flag had the last cold, windy Colorado winter Mochi spent at Sand Creek with her family before they were killed.

Figure 1.3.   Chief Black Kettle (bottom row, second from left), leader of the
South Cheyenne, raised the American flag over their camp in an effort to stop the
attack at Sand Creek. The Denver Public Library, Western History Collection, X-
32364

2

THE REVEREND COLONEL

The smell of the sandy beaches and seawater of the southern Florida peninsula was in sharp contrast to the sweet aroma of the rolling plains and crystal clear rivers of northern Colorado. Fort Marion was unlike any place Mochi had ever been in her life. The Spanish once lived in and ruled the oceanfront outpost.[1] No matter where Indian prisoners were within the garrison they found reminders of Spain constantly beckoning them to behold her ancient glory. For a long while Mochi stood in the shadow of the walls of the fort, lost in thought. Soldiers in towers at the corners of the rampart watched her with careful eyes in case she tried to escape.[2]

Fort Marion was surrounded by a moat. Two drawbridges extended to the other side and provided people with a way to cross. Below the bridges and the casements were miles of dungeons. No sooner had Mochi and the other Indian prisoners arrived than the soldiers began telling tales of the skeletons found chained to the walls, warning the condemned Cheyenne that they would suffer the same fate if they caused trouble.[3] Mochi took the threat seriously. It had been her experience that white men never made good on any promise to the Indian apart from those of injury or death. Respected Cheyenne elders had foreseen all that would happen to the Indian people.

When she was a girl, Mochi had begun hearing stories of what was to happen to the Indian. Her grandparents shared tales of a prophet and teacher named Sweet Medicine who warned the Cheyenne that they would be overtaken.[4] According to the traditional folklore, Sweet Medicine told his people that only the rocks and mountains were forever and that the "Indians would be like dust on the prairie." He shared with those around him during his last hours on earth:

> I've seen in my mind that sometime after I am dead they will come. Light-skinned, bearded men will arrive with sticks spitting fire. They will conquer the land and drive the Indian before them. They will kill the animals who give their flesh that Indians may live, and they will bring strange animals for them to ride and eat. They will introduce war and evil, strange sicknesses and death. They will take the Indians' land little by little, until there is nothing left. You must be strong when that time comes, you men, and particularly you women, because much depends on you, because you are the perpetuators of life and if you weaken, the Cheyenne will cease to be. [5]

For a time Mochi's life in the land of her ancestors on the Great Plains was without sorrow or harsh struggle. She contented herself with doing what was traditionally required of Cheyenne women. Using long branches filled with dried leaves, she swept the dirt from the lodge where she lived with her husband, gathered wood to make fires, and collected the daily water. She prepared the food her husband brought home and made moccasins and robes with the buffalo and deer hides. Mochi was responsible, as were all Cheyenne women, for keeping track of the family belongings; the Cheyenne lifestyle could be quite transitory. Mochi's job was to break camp, pack, and reassemble the lodge once a new location was determined. [6]

Mochi's grandmother and those before her believed the role of the Cheyenne woman was set by the Wise One Above, or as the Cheyenne referred to him, He'amave' ho'e. [7] According to Cheyenne legend the Wise One Above made both man and woman. Cheyenne ancestors told their children:

> When the Wise One Above made the man in the south, he took from his own right side a rib to make him with, and when he made the woman in the north, he took from the man's left side a rib to make her of. Wise One Above then stood between those two with his back toward the rising sun. When he placed them apart he spoke to them and said, "In that direction," pointing to the south where the man was, "you will find all kinds of animals and birds different from those which you find in that direction." Pointing to the north where the

woman was he said, "The birds that live in the south will come to the north in the summer time. Where the woman is it will be cold, and you will freeze and the grass and the trees will not grow well. There will be hardly any at all of them. But where the man is, everything will grow, grass, bushes and timber.

The woman who had been made and placed in the north will never grow any older. The woman in the north controls Ho-im-a-ha, commonly interpreted as 'winter man' or 'storm,' the power that brings the cold and snow. He obeys her and she will care for the man the Wise One Above made and she will help in defending theirs and make it storm if there is cause.[8]

When Mochi's family and homeland were eventually threatened she did as the stories of the elders told her the woman should do: defend it and make it storm.[9]

It was raining on June 18, 1864, when a frantic lone rider spurred his galloping horse toward Fort Lyon, Colorado. After making sure the man was neither a Cheyenne nor an Arapaho Indian, army soldiers on guard opened the gate of the fort and let him in. "The red devils have massacred a whole family on Running Creek," the desperate rider exclaimed.[10] The commander of the outpost managed to calm the man down long enough for him to explain that a band of Arapaho Indians had attacked a ranch twenty-five miles east of the fort. Nathan Hungate, his wife, and two children had been killed in the raid. Their bodies were mutilated and burned in a fire that destroyed the ranch house. Angry freight wagon drivers transported the mangled bodies to Denver for everyone to see. The public was outraged and insisted that the government needed to intervene and protect the settlers on the plains from the Indians.[11]

Colorado Governor John Evans called an emergency meeting with territory leaders and army officers. Denver was placed under martial law, and volunteer units were called to help fight the Arapaho warriors involved with the Hungate massacre.[12] Colonel John M. Chivington was one of the men Governor Evans consulted about exercising such extreme measures.[13] Known as the "Fighting Parson," Chivington was a frontier preacher turned soldier. He was born in Warren County, Ohio, on January 27, 1821. His father, Isaac, and mother, Jane, carved out a home for themselves in the wilderness twenty miles northeast of Cincinnati. The couple struggled against the elements, wildlife, and Shawnee Indians to keep the land they occupied. Isaac and Jane had four children: three sons and one daughter. John was a middle child. His mother taught him how to read and write, and his father taught him how to be a woodsman. [14]

According to historical records from the Kansas Historical Society, Chivington was an imposing figure. In March 1902, his friend John Speer described him in a letter as "a man of fine personal appearance." Chivington was six feet four and a half inches tall and weighed 265 pounds. "His father was six feet six inches tall," Speer wrote in his memoirs. "The Chivington family was all large." [15]

When John was eight years old, he took over marketing the family timber business. He spent a considerable amount of time working in Cincinnati, where he met his wife Martha Rollason. Martha was from Virginia and worked in the city as a servant girl in the home of some of her friends. She was two years older than Chivington, short, proficient in French, and an expert seamstress. The two married in late 1840. Early on Chivington supported his wife by working as a carpenter. The couple attended the Methodist church in southern Ohio, and by 1842 John decided he wanted to enter the ministry. In September 1844, Chivington was ordained as a Methodist preacher. His first assignment was at a church in Goshen, Ohio. [16]

An influx of rowdy and rough men traveling through the region on the way west created a great deal of unrest in the area where Chivington preached. There was drinking and prostitution, gunfighting and gambling, and the need for reform was evident. Chivington not only spoke out against such immoral behavior but also helped law enforcement officials restore law and order. The big man with the big voice and personality gained a reputation as a fighter. Not only did the community respect him, but it also had a healthy fear of him.

Encouraged by the changes made in the unruly community, Chivington reasoned his services would be well received in other towns. In 1848, his wife and three children moved to Quincy, Illinois. As a leader in the Methodist Episcopal Church, he assisted in ending disputes between neighbors and kept his flock safe from the criminal elements by putting a stop to their misdeeds and carting them to jail. Chivington and Martha helped establish schools and curtail drinking at public events such as picnics and horse races. [17]

After less than a year in Quincy, Chivington and his family were transferred to the Methodist church in Pleasant Green, Missouri. The itinerant preacher served five churches in western Missouri and was a

Figure 2.1.   Colonel John M. Chivington, the fighting parson, Civil War hero and leader of the attack on Sand Creek. The Denver Public Library, Western History Collection, Z-128

missionary to the Wyandot Indians in Kansas City, Kansas.[18] The Wyandot Indians had been forced to the area by the government. Their native homeland was along the Ohio River, but settlers pushed the Indians out of the region. Life in Kansas was becoming increasingly difficult for them as once again they were being crowded off the spot said to be reserved for them. Chivington took on the task of easing tension between the Wyandot and settlers encroaching on their space. Using an interpreter, he was able to reason with the Indians and share the gospel. Many converted to Christianity and helped Chivington build a church near their village.[19]

Chivington spent time with the white settlers educating them about the Indians. He was able to change the perception many pioneers had that the Wyandot were savages. In time they came to accept one another and work side-by-side farming and trading produce.[20]

In 1854, Chivington was transferred to a parish in St. Joseph, Missouri. St. Joseph had a reputation as one of the toughest cities in the country. Hundreds of people passed through the river port en route to the trails leading west. Saloons and gambling halls flanked the thoroughfares. Unsuspecting travelers were victims of highway robbers and stray bullets from gunfights. Once Chivington improved the quality of the local schools, he set to work reforming the city. Dressed in ministerial garb complete with white shirt and black collar, Chivington took to the streets, preaching to individuals most vulnerable to the vices all around. He was successful in closing down a few bars and escorting out of town those people who refused to succumb to the ways of polite society. St. Joseph remained a respectable community for more than eight years. Chivington's presence helped keep order.[21]

When rumors of a possible Civil War reached St. Joseph in 1860, Chivington was not shy about telling his congregation that slavery was wrong. People who were opposed to his view sent threatening notes to the parson. He was warned not only to stop preaching in St. Joseph but also to stop preaching anywhere in Platte County, Missouri.[22] He was warned that he'd be tarred and feathered if he said anything against slavery. Chivington was not intimidated. The Sunday following the warning he stepped up to the pulpit carrying two pistols. After laying a gun down on each side of his Bible he announced, "By the grace of God and these two revolvers I'm going to preach here today." Chivington proceeded without interruption. Chivington's friends seemed to recognize the trouble to which he had opened himself. Fearing that Chivington's life was in serious danger from pro-slavery groups, his friends persuaded him to take his family to the new position the church wanted him to take. By the fall of 1856, Chivington was appointed presiding elder of the churches in the Kansas and Nebraska regions. [23]

After two years in Omaha, Chivington was transferred to Nebraska City and was given the job of organizing the local district of the church and clearing out the negative influences that were poisoning the area. Proclaiming that he was operating on the authority of God, Chivington destroyed cases of rum and whiskey some residents had been stockpiling and strongly urged all residents to attend church. [24]

From Nebraska City, Chivington moved with his wife and children to the Rocky Mountain District, where he had accepted an assignment as elder. It was March 1860, and a flood of humanity was parading to the Colorado gold fields and specifically to Pike's Peak. [25] He built a home for himself and his family in Denver and then set about gathering believers to help him construct a church. The First Methodist Church in the rugged territory was a small but adequate building. From this location Chivington dispatched missionaries to carry the Lord's message to mining camps and other settlements in his district. By the beginning of summer in 1860, a considerable degree of order had been restored to the lawless mining burg, and hundreds of prospectors were attending church and taking communion.

The Civil War began on April 12, 1861, but John Chivington did not join in the fighting until nearly two years after the first shot. The Methodist Church did not want to lose one of its most effective ministers. Committees were formed by southern supporters to keep clergymen like Chivington from speaking out against their fight with the north. Chivington could not be kept quiet. He told a congregation before him at the funeral of a Union recruit: "I am a man of lawful age and full size, and was an American citizen before I became a minister. If the church had required me to renounce my rights of manhood or American citizenship before I became a minister, I should have respectfully declined." [26]

Shortly after the First Colorado Volunteer Cavalry Regiment was formed, Chivington offered his services. He declined an appointment as chaplain for the regiment and requested a combat post. Newly elected governor of Colorado William Gilpin honored Chivington's request and appointed him a major over the First Colorado Regiment. [27] Chivington's military experience was limited to a few months of service in a militia company in Ohio and reading numerous books on the subject of military history and tactics. Chivington's natural leadership ability prompted officers around him to place him in charge of training soldiers for service. He eventually rose in rank to colonel. He led more than four hundred volunteers through the Battle of Glorieta Pass. The confrontation involved a showdown between a scattered Union and Confederate forces that had campaigned in New Mexico, one alert watching for blue or gray uniforms and the other watching for Apache and Navajo warriors. Union forces won the battle, captured Albuquerque, and occupied it during the summer of 1863.[28]

Chivington proved himself to be an effective military officer. Acting quickly against enemy troops, Chivington and the First Colorado Regiment managed to overtake Confederate soldiers and confiscate their supply train and cannons at a crucial time in the battle. He was well respected by his superiors and troops alike.[29]

Chivington's regiment returned to Colorado in January 1863. The small number of troops under the colonel's command was the only organized defense against hostile Indians in the territory. The job of the regiment was to protect the areas of eastern Colorado and western Kansas. They were kept quite busy during the spring and summer of 1863 dealing with a number of Indian raids on settlers. Property was stolen, livestock was driven off, and people were killed. The Indians were pushing back against the boundary-less white men. The Sioux, Arapaho, and Cheyenne combined forces to rid their land of further invasions. The job securing the plains eventually became overwhelming.[30]

Political and military leaders in Nebraska and Colorado quickly informed Washington of the predicament, and help came by way of two Indian agents. The agents were married to Arapaho women and had the ear of both Cheyenne and Arapaho Indian chiefs. The agents were instructed to negotiate a peace treaty with the warring Indians. None of the Indians from the combined tribes would agree to any of the United States proposals for peace.[31] Colonel Chivington was appalled at their obstinacy and their unrelenting assault on westward pioneers. Cheyenne Dog Soldiers defied every attempt by Chivington and his regiment to stop numerous raids. Only the youngest and strongest members of the tribe were Dog Soldiers. According to historian and author Robert H. Lowie, Cheyenne Dog Soldiers were "ambitious men who enjoyed torturing and killing and believed that old age was evil and to die young in battle a point of honor."

Figure 2.2.   Colorado Governor John Evans was implicated in creating the conditions for the Sand Creek Massacre. The Denver Public Library, Western History
Collection, Z-2873

Colonel Chivington believed the Dog Soldiers were an enemy that could only be defeated by complete annihilation.[32]

Throughout the summer of 1864, Colorado Territorial Governor John Evans sent urgent messages to various military and civilian authorities asking for additional troops to help in the Plains Indian War. In mid-August approval was given by military personnel in Washington, D.C., to recruit volunteers to aide in the fighting. Colonel Chivington was in charge of dispatching these troops to points along the Overland Trail where many wagon trains and stagecoaches had been overtaken by Indians. Chivington and his volunteers managed to bring about some order with a small band of Cheyenne and Arapaho who initially refused to enter into a treaty with the government.[33]

On September 4, 1864, Chief Black Kettle delivered a written message to the garrison at Fort Lyon expressing that all the Plains Indians, specifically the Southern Cheyenne, Kiowa, and Arapaho, wanted to talk peace. "All have come to the conclusion to make peace with you, provided you make peace with us," Black Kettle's note read. "We have several prisoners of yours which we are willing to give up providing you give up yours."[34]

Military officers along with more than two dozen armed troops agreed to meet with Black Kettle and other tribal chiefs to discuss a conference to be held in Denver to negotiate terms of a peace agreement. The conference was held on September 28, 1864, outside Denver at Camp Weld. Among the Indian leaders participating in the summit were White Antelope, chief of the Cheyenne; Bull Bear, chief of the Cheyenne Dog Soldiers; Arapaho Chief Left Hand's brother, Neva; and several other minor chiefs of both tribes. The United States was represented by Governor John Evans, Colonel George Shoup, Major E. W. Wynkoop, Indian agent Simeon Whitely, Colonel John M. Chivington, and several private citizens.[35]

The Indian leaders admitted their animosity toward the white man and why they felt as they did. Black Kettle assured all present that the tribes wanted to live in harmony if possible. Colonel Chivington told the chiefs that peace could only happen when and if all the hostile members of the Plains Nations, specifically the Cheyenne and Arapaho Indians, surrendered. There were still many Indian warriors who refused to stop raids on army posts and settlers. "My rule of fighting white men or Indians is to fight them until they lay down their arms and submit to military author-

ity," Colonel Chivington announced. Compliance with Colonel Chivington's terms was not immediate. Black Kettle and a large contingent of
Cheyenne Indians were among those who would eventually follow the
colonel's directives.[36]

More than six hundred Indians, including Black Kettle, set up camp
thirty-five miles from Fort Lyon on Sand Creek.[37] In mid-November a
winter storm broke over the region, covering the encampment with snow.
Mochi, her family, and the other Indians believed Winter Man would stay
in the Cheyenne country for several months.[38] According to Cheyenne
legend, Winter Man liked to sweep over the people gathered around
campfire, feasting and singing. It made him angry to see the Indian happy. It also made him angry to see anyone besides the Indian on the prairie.
Winter Man wanted the Cheyenne to remember the power he ultimately
had to send snow and drive animals into hiding from his fury.[39] Mochi's
father and grandfather told her that Winter Man had brought the violent
snowstorm in the winter of 1864 to protest the Cheyenne alliance with the
white man.[40] Black Kettle and his band of Cheyenne were willing to risk
antagonizing Winter Man in exchange for peace between the Indians and
the flood of newcomers claiming their native homeland.

3

TERMS OF SURRENDER

Silence hung taut and crystal clear over Denver, where Colonel Chivington and the First and Third Colorado Cavalry were stationed one morning in early November 1864. The regiments were bored, cold, and frustrated. They had joined the call to arms to put an end to the actions of hostile Indians against those who sought to expand the western territory.[1] The Plains Indians, which included the Arapaho, Cheyenne, Kiowa, Pawnee, Sioux, and Ute, were standing in the way of the economic growth of the United States, and the army had been instructed to remedy the situation. Members of the First and Third Colorado Cavalry were anxious to get the job done and go home, but the frigid weather had brought their plans to a halt.[2]

Although Black Kettle and his band of Cheyenne had agreed to discuss peace, Colonel Chivington and other officers such as Major Scott Anthony felt the Indians had not fully complied with the conditions set by the military for talk of peace to even begin.[3] A number of warring Cheyenne and Arapaho tribes had not agreed to surrender all their weapons or their horses to the government.[4] The Indian horse was an incredibly hardy animal which could endure the winter months better than cavalry horses.[5] Men such as Chivington knew if the Indians were to be conquered it was essential that their horses be confiscated in order to keep them from riding to future raids and attacks.[6] Chivington and Major Anthony questioned the sincerity of Black Kettle and the other Indian leaders regarding total surrender and suspected their motivation was winter temperatures and lack of food.[7]

The army initially provided supplies to the Indian tribes living at Sand Creek that were willing to consider peace, but after a while those supplies dwindled and Major Anthony turned the Indians away. He returned the limited weapons that had been confiscated, too, and told the Indians they needed to return to the prairie to hunt. [8] The military's behavior made the Cheyenne and Arapaho more wary of the United States government's word. They now believed soldiers would follow after them and attack. [9]

Colonel Chivington was preoccupied with the morale of his troops and the fact that their enlistments were almost completed. [10] Whatever action was going to be taken against the Indians had to be done soon, or there would be no soldiers left to aid in a fight. While considering the options before him, Chivington reviewed a directive he had issued on November 9, 1863, which read, "All persons whomsoever within the District of Colorado are strictly forbidden to sell or give away to any Indians living within or who may visit the bounds of the District, any powder, lead or gun caps until further notice. Any person violating this order will be deemed guilty of military offense and will be dealt with accordingly." [11] As far as Colonel Chivington knew, the order had not been violated, but the troops were tired of the enforcement of the directive being their side job. Soldiers whose enlistment had almost run out reminded their commanding officer to "use them or lose them." Chivington felt pressed to do just that. [12]

The more time passed the more anxious Chivington became. He imagined a full-scale invasion of settlements and forts in the region by Dog Soldiers. He wrote letters to his superiors and his wife expressing his concern that if the Indians he referred to as "red rebels" were not held accountable for their uncivilized behavior they would never stop. [13]

Chivington was not alone in thinking that the Plains Indians were murderers who should be killed, imprisoned, or defeated through force. Both Major S. G. Colley of the Upper Arkansas Indian Agency and Colonel George Shoup agreed the Indians were problematic and needed to answer for their hostile acts. The officers all believed that "no lasting peace could be made until all the Indians were severely punished." [14]

One of the most egregious acts the Indians perpetrated was on the women captured by war parties. [15] According to the book *Massacre of the Mountains* by J. P. Dunn, women were treated particularly badly by Plains Indians. A woman captive was considered common property of all the warriors and was raped nightly until the Indians reached their village.

At that point the woman became sole property of the one who captured her. She was often sold or gambled away to another tribe. If the woman resisted, her arms and legs were tied to four pegs driven into the ground to prevent her from struggling. She was beaten, mutilated, or even killed for resisting. If a woman continued to try to escape after such treatment, she was maimed so as to ensure death in case of rescue and left to die slowly.[16]

White men who captured Indian women often raped their victims as well, but Indian women rarely gave their testimonies to anyone who could make the attackers answer for their offenses.[17]

General Patrick Conner, commander of the military district of Utah, left Colonel Chivington with the impression that the Secretary of War had sent him to find out if the campaign against the Indians was being conducted as it should be. After his meeting with Chivington, General Conner made a comment that fueled Chivington's notion that the government wanted the situation with the Indians handled once and for all. "I think from the temper of the men that you have, and all I can learn, that you will give these Indians a most terrible thrashing if you can catch them," General Conner told Chivington. "If it was in the mountains and you had them in a canyon with escape cut off, you could catch them; but I'm afraid on these plains you won't do it."[18] Chivington assured the general that he and his troops were prepared to do what was needed and told him that he would contact the general with the result of their encounter with the warring tribes.[19]

On November 23, 1864, Colonel Chivington rallied his troops together and traveled to Fort Lyon, where he assumed command of an expedition to seek out and attack hostile Plains Indians. Chivington had no official orders to embark on the mission, and he was reminded of that by a few officers under him.[20] Captain Charles Soule reminded the colonel that peaceful Indians were expecting the government to honor the agreement to protect them and see that they were not attacked. Convinced there were no peaceful Indians, Chivington dismissed the warning and proceeded with his plan to annihilate them.[21]

Fearful that word of the intention of the expedition would be leaked to the Indians, Colonel Chivington intercepted all travelers along the route to and from Fort Lyon. He took pioneers and traders into temporary custody and left detachments of guards at all ranches and settlements. He also ordered a picket around the fort to prevent anyone leaving without authorization.[22]

Major Anthony supported Chivington's safeguard measures and expressed his gratitude to the officers for being there. "Damn glad you've come, Colonel!" Anthony later recalled saying. "I've got a band of hostiles only forty miles from here and have been waiting for assistance in dealing with them."[23] Chivington and his staff, Major Anthony and Major S. G. Colley of the Upper Arkansas Indian Agency, met at the post headquarters to discuss a plan of action. In the meeting Major Anthony was asked to elaborate on the whereabouts of the Indians. Anthony explained that there was a band of more than one thousand Indians encamped on Sand Creek forty miles to the north. "Mostly Cheyenne under Chief Black Kettle," Anthony added, "with a few Arapaho, and another group of about two thousand more Cheyenne on the Smoky Hill, sixty to seventy miles further north." Major Anthony went on to tell the officers that the Cheyenne had rejected an offer of peace and that there was every indication the Indians would attack the post. Major Colley confirmed Major Anthony's assessment of the situation and explained to Colonel Chivington, "I have done everything in my power to make them behave themselves, but for the past six months I have been able to do nothing with them. In my opinion, they should be punished for their hostile acts."[24]

After hearing what others had to say about the matter, Colonel Chivington made the decision to confront the Indians. According to federal court documents, Colonel Chivington informed Major Anthony that he was going to march to Sand Creek.[25] Anthony offered to be a part of the march and volunteered the 125 men in his command to accompany them. He advised Colonel Chivington to surround the Sand Creek camp so that no one could escape and alert the main band of Cheyenne on the Smoky Hill about what was happening. Anthony felt this strategy would give Indians and agents in the camp the opportunity to escape before any fighting began. Among those Anthony believed were friendly and interested in peace were Black Kettle and Left Hand. Chivington was not convinced they were sincere about living harmoniously under the government's rule.[26] The colonel recalled:

> Black Kettle is the principle chief of the Cheyenne nation which has
> been engaged in bloody war with whites since April [1864]. His claim

of friendship seems to have arisen with the ending of the summer season and the approach of cold weather when Indians fight at a disadvantage. However, it is not my intention to attack without warning. Actual operations must, of course, depend upon conditions which we find on arrival, but I propose to first immobilize the Indians, if possible, and then to offer them a parley on terms of surrender. Such terms would include the delivering up for punishment of all savages guilty of hostilities, the return of all stolen properties, the surrender of all firearms and the giving of hostages to ensure against further hostilities. [27]

Chivington and Anthony combined their efforts to choreograph a precise plan of attack. It was decided that a number of howitzers would be used in the expedition. The powerful artillery pieces were used to propel shells at high angles and were much more forceful than a rifle. The post quartermaster provided the ammunition and rations needed for the impending battle. The troops were assembled and informed that they would be leaving at once for Sand Creek. [28]

Captain Soule again raised an objection to the attack. His sentiments were echoed by Major Wynkoop, an officer at Fort Lyon who had successfully negotiated a surrender of the hostages the Cheyenne had taken in early 1864. The two men felt that Black Kettle and the band of Indians he oversaw deserved to be thanked for their cooperation and exempted from any raid. [29]

Lieutenant Joseph Cramer, one of Chivington's men, attempted to reason with Chivington and persuade him to abandon the idea of invading the Indian camps along Sand Creek. Chivington refused to listen and threatened Lieutenant Cramer with a court martial if he went against his commanding officer. "The Cheyenne Nation has been waging bloody war against the whites," Chivington reminded Lieutenant Cramer. "They have been guilty of robbery, arson, murder, rape, and fiendish torture, not even sparing women and little children. I believe it right and honorable to use any means under God's heaven to kill Indians who kill and torture children and women. Damn any man who is in sympathy with them." [30]

"I will obey your orders," Lieutenant Cramer told Chivington, "but only under protest. I feel it would be murder to attack those Indians." [31]

The final march to Sand Creek began at eight o'clock at night on November 28, 1864. Colonel Chivington led 750 soldiers across the trackless prairie. Motivated by vengeance and the desire to prove himself to government officials who had criticized him for his inability to restrain the Indians, Chivington was resolved to give the Cheyenne and Arapaho leaders and their bands a lesson they would remember.[32]

Major Anthony's Indian scout acted as guide for the troops. It was a cold, cloudless night, and the men took turns walking and trotting their horses on the route the Indian was leading them. When they were eight to ten miles from the Indian camp the march was brought to a halt. Chivington was annoyed. He had given orders that the expedition would keep moving until its objective was accomplished. The guide defended his decision to stop, telling Chivington that there was a risk of the Indians hearing them if they continued. "Wolf he howl, Injun dog he hear wolf and dog howl too; Injun he hear dog and listen, hear something and run off," the guide explained.[33]

Chivington was suspicious of the guide. "I haven't had an Indian to eat for a long time," Chivington snapped at the guide. "If you fool with me and don't lead us to that camp, I'll have you for breakfast." Not long after the verbal altercation the guide urged his horse onward. The troops followed after him. No one spoke or slowed down until dawn, when they reached a ridge overlooking a sprawling valley. Below them in the far distance were the Indian camps.[34]

The Cheyenne camps lay in a horseshoe bend of Sand Creek north of an almost dry streambed. Black Kettle's tepee was near the center of the village, and the tepee of White Antelope, one of the leaders of the Dog Soldiers, was to the west. Indians under the leadership of Cheyenne Chief War Bonnet were situated to the west of the camp as well. On the east side, slightly separated from the Cheyenne, was Left Hand's Arapaho camp. All together there were about six hundred Indians in the creek bend; two-thirds of them were women and children. Most of the warriors were several miles to the east, hunting buffalo.[35]

The Indians, asleep in their lodges, were unaware that trouble was on the horizon. Black Kettle and the other Indian leaders were so confident all was well and would remain so that they did not keep a night watch. The morning was quiet. Mochi and the other women in the tribe awoke before sunrise to begin gathering firewood and preparing the morning meal. Infants and small children were cared for, and Mochi helped mothers with the chore. She didn't have any children of her own but knew when the time came the other women would help her when needed. With the exception of the herd of Cheyenne ponies on the south bank of the Sand Creek that were acting a bit anxious, there was nothing out of the ordinary. Mochi carried on with her duties, concerned for nothing apart from feeding her family and keeping them warm.[36]

The peaceful morning was reminiscent of a morning in a story the elders told of two warriors named Sweet Medicine and Standing-on-the-Ground. Both men arrived on a serene setting where the Cheyenne people were playing a game. Both men were painted and dressed alike. Sweet Medicine claimed the paint he wore was medicine paint and had great powers. Standing-on-the-Ground said that the paint he wore was given to him by Ma-ta-ma, the old woman that lived in the water, and he added that the paint was spiritual paint. Standing-on-the-Ground accused Sweet Medicine of lying about the origin of his paint and demanded proof he was telling the truth. Sweet Medicine accused Standing-on-the-Ground of being a spy who copied Sweet Medicine's way of dressing.[37]

A decision was made within the tribe that both men should go to see Ma-ta-ma so she could prove who was telling the truth. The men agreed and met with the old woman that lived in the water and told her of their dispute. She was wise and stern and was pleased they had come to see her. "You both have something to learn," Ma-ta-ma told them, "and I will teach you. You think of your pride and not the people."[38]

Ma-ta-ma served them a meal and challenged them to eat what had been prepared without arguing. She also encouraged them to eat all they wanted. The more the men ate, the more food appeared on their plates. "See, there is plenty for both," Ma-ta-ma pointed out. "That is the way it is with spiritual power. Watch, and I will give you new paint." She painted each of them with red, all over, and on each she painted the sun and the moon, in yellow. Then she tied a feather from the eagle's wing, painted red, in the scalp lock of each young man. "This is the way you are to dress from now on," she said.[39]

Then, while they sat with Ma-ta-ma and listened to her words, she showed them many wonderful things. The walls of the room seemed to disappear, and as far as the eye could see, to the left was a great herd of buffalo, blackening the prairie there were so many. To the right there were great fields of green growing corn, and to the back was a herd of horses, pawing and stamping. She told them what these were and how they would serve the people in days to come, for they were new.[40]

Figure 3.1.   This drawing shows the relative locations of Cheyenne tepees and the members of the Colorad~
~e start of the battle of Sand Creek. The Denver Public Library, Western History Collection, X-33806

Then she showed them people fighting, and when they looked more closely they saw themselves among the fighters, dressed and painted red with the sun and moon in yellow and the red feather in their scalp locks, just as they were then.[41]

"You see, you will fight together," she said, "and you will win, if you will heed my words." Then she taught them many things that would be helpful to the people. They listened carefully, remembering what she taught. Then she gave a dish of meat to Sweet Medicine.

"This is your proof," she said. "Take it to the Cheyenne. Tell them, too, that when the sun goes down, I will send the buffalo back."[42]

She gave a dish of cooked corn to Standing-on-the-Ground. "Take this food to the Cheyenne," she said. "It will prove your words." She gave him seed corn and taught him how it was to be planted and cared for. "Tell them they must guard the corn for seven years. They must not give it away or allow it to be stolen. If they fail, it will be bad for them."[43]

The corn was planted and grew, and the buffalo did come. According to the legend this was to show the Indians that the Cheyenne leaders should always see that the old people and the orphan children were fed and cared for. When morning came, Sweet Medicine and Standing-on-the-Ground placed a tobacco offering on a disk of red stone. They then went out and surrounded the herd of buffalo and killed a great many. When they had enough, Sweet Medicine made them stop killing, and the women dressed the meat and prepared the skins for robes and moccasins.[44]

That night they had a great feast, and the story of what Ma-ta-ma had taught Sweet Medicine and Standing-on-the-Ground was told again and again. Night turned into day; all was quiet and still, and everyone was confident it would stay that way.[45]

At daybreak on November 29, 1864, the sound of the drumming of hooves on the sand flats interrupted the hushed routine of the Indian women and children. Some of the women believed it was only buffalo running hard in the near distance. Neither Mochi nor any of the other members of the tribes along the Sand Creek were alarmed. They went about their duties oblivious to any danger.[46]

4

NOTHING LIVES LONG

Colonel John Chivington and representatives of the First and Third Colorado Cavalry rode hard and fast from the sun-touched butte where they'd been waiting at the Indian encampment along Sand Creek. A bugler sounded the charge as the horses' hooves drummed and the soldiers shouted, reins in their teeth and guns in their fists.[1] Members of the Cheyenne and Arapaho tribes living in the path of the cavalry hurried from their lodges and frantically scattered in different directions. Mothers scooped young children into their arms and ushered elderly men and women to clusters of trees. Braves grabbed weapons in order to defend themselves from the surprise invasion.[2]

Several of Chivington's troops raced to the paddock where the Indians' horses were corralled. Without the herd the Indians would be at a disadvantage, unable to pursue attackers or flee from the chaos. Just before the flood of soldiers arrived on the scene, Colonel Chivington urged his men to "recall the blood of wives and children spilled on the Platte and Arkansas [Rivers]."[3]

The full force of the cavalry's strike yielded immediate devastation. Bullet-ridden children fell where they once played; mothers lay dying with their babies in their arms; elderly women and men collapsed from gunshot wounds in their backs. It was a killing frenzy. Some Indians managed to escape without injury and take refuge in thick brush and behind scattered rock outcroppings.[4]

Figure 4.1.   The massacre at Sand Creek, Colorado between United States troops and Cheyenne. Women panic behind the trees in the foreground, while warriors and soldiers fight among tepees in the background. Public Library, Western History Collection, X-33805

Black Kettle tried desperately to keep his people from panicking. He clung to the belief that the attack would cease when the soldiers noticed the American flag unfurled. He and Chief White Antelope huddled at the base of the flag post. They only ran for cover when they realized the soldiers were hell-bent on annihilating them. [5]

Fearless Cheyenne women and braves stood their ground, refusing to leave without a fight. The men exchanged shots with the soldiers and the women fought using spears and knives, all of which gave members of the tribe a chance to retreat slowly up the dried streambed. Many Cheyenne and Arapaho were killed as they ran to hide in the banks of the Sand Creek. [6]

Indian horses spooked by gunfire broke away from the soldiers trying to drive them from the encampment. Indian women who managed to capture and calm a horse long enough to climb onto its back were shot. Their lifeless bodies slid from the backs of the horses onto the hard earth. Braves on foot who dared charge the relentless soldiers were stopped in their tracks with a barrage of bullets. [7] According to accounts from those who witnessed the battle, children who ventured out of hiding waving white flags and mothers who pleaded for their infants' lives were beaten with the butt of the soldiers' guns and then scalped.

Black Kettle stood watching the bloody event in disbelief. He made a white flag of truce and raised it under the American flag. It had no effect upon the soldiers. Chivington's persistent orders to continue to pursue the enemy were strictly followed. Black Kettle grabbed his wife, and the two fled toward a creek bed. The bark of the rifles all around him was steady, and there seemed to be no escape for the Cheyenne leader. Black Kettle's wife was struck by several bullets, and the concussion of the shots knocked her face-first onto the ground. Black Kettle tried to get her onto her feet again, but her injuries were too serious. The cavalry was bearing down on him quickly and he was forced to leave his wife's body behind. He continued running until he reached the sandy creek bed. He hid in the dry wash under a thick overgrowth of brush. [8]

White Antelope attempted to halt the attack by raising his arms in the air and shouting in English for the troops to stop. His plea went unanswered. "Nothing lives long," he could be heard saying as the soldiers pressed on toward him, "only the earth and the mountains." [9] An overzealous soldier rode up to the seventy-three-year-old chief and shot him to death at point blank range. The soldier then dismounted his horse, removed a knife from the canvas belt around his waist, and proceeded to scalp and dismember White Antelope's body. He cut off the Indian's nose, ears, and genitalia. [10]

Mochi was among the numerous Indians frantic to escape the slaughter. She watched her mother get shot in the head and heard the cries of her father and husband as they fought for their lives. Mesmerized by the carnage erupting around her, she paused briefly to consider what was happening. In that moment of reflection one of Chivington's soldiers rode toward her. She stared at him as he quickly approached, her face mirroring shock and dismay. She heard a slug sing viciously past her head. The soldier jumped off his ride and attacked her. Mochi fought back hard and eventually broke free from the soldier's grip. Before the man could start after her again she grabbed a gun lying on the ground near her, fired, and killed him. [11]

The Sand Creek Massacre reached an end at four o'clock in the afternoon on November 29, 1864. [12] When Colonel Chivington and his men put away their weapons, a grim stillness hung in the air. Apart from the sound of suffering from wounded and dying Indians and horses being driven away from the encampment, all was deathly quiet. More than one hundred Indians had been killed in the raid. The First Colorado Cavalry had lost only seven men. The temporary cease-fire was interrupted by a mammoth blaze. Chivington had ordered all the lodges in the Indian camp burned to the ground. He didn't want any of the Arapaho or Cheyenne leaders who survived to return to the encampment and reestablish the area as their base. [13]

Prior to the blaze being ignited, Chivington and his troops searched through the Indians' belongings. Among the items were clothing, pictures, and jewelry taken from settlers and their wagon trains during raids by the Indians. [14]

Long after night had fallen, survivors of the massacre crawled out of the brush in the creek beds. It was bitter cold, and blood had frozen over their wounds. The only thought in their minds was to flee eastward toward Smoky Hill and join the warriors from other tribes.

According to George Bent, a Cheyenne-American and former Confederate soldier who was living at Black Kettle's camp during the Sand Creek Massacre, the journey to Smoky Hill was a struggle for the survivors of the bloody battle. "It was a terrible march," George wrote in his memoirs, "most of us being on foot, without food, ill-clad and encumbered with women and children." The survivors traveled fifty miles to their destination. "As we approached the camp there was a terrible scene," George later wrote. "Everyone was crying, even the warriors, and the women and children were screaming and wailing. Nearly everyone present had lost some relatives or friends, and many of them in their grief were gashing themselves with knives until the blood flowed in streams."[15]

News of the horrible massacre and the lead role Chivington played in it traveled quickly from Denver to points east of the Mississippi. Officials associated with the war department such as Major General Alexander McCook, commander of Fort Leavenworth, Kansas, called the atrocity one of the most "cold-blooded, revolting, and diabolical ever conceived by man or devil."[16] Major General McCook was assigned by the government the duty of investigating the Sand Creek Massacre. Having fought against the Indians in several campaigns, he was experienced in their tactics, character, and disposition. The war department considered his assessment of the matter to be valuable and unbiased.

According to the September 8, 1865, edition of the *Delphi Weekly Times*, "the sworn account of witnesses of the affair is enough to make any man blush for his species." The news article continued,

> It was an indiscriminant, wholesale murder of men, women and children, accompanied by the disfigurement of dead bodies of both sexes in every revolting and sickening form and manner. Unborn babies were torn from the womb of dying mothers and scalped. Children of the most tender age were butchered, soldiers adorned their hats with portions of the bodies of both males and females, and the flag and uniform of the United States were disgraced by acts of fiendish barbarity, so revolting in their details that a truthful account cannot be published in a respectable journal without giving offense to decency. And all these atrocities were committed on a band of Indians, who had voluntarily entrusted themselves to the protection of the government, received assurances of care, and who had flying above the encampment at that time a white flag given to them with the promise that this was to be to them security and guardianship as long as they remained under it and continued to be friendly.
>
> These Indians were under the leadership of "Black Kettle," a chief whose friendship for the whites had been proverbial for years. He brought the men, women and children of his tribe together to live near the fort, and under the care of the whites. His trust was repaid by

indiscriminant massacre; his friendship was rewarded by outrage on the living and disfigurement of the dead; his confidence requited by betrayal, and by murder, so sickening in its form that it passes all understanding to imagine how anyone could have executed it.

All these facts are established by sworn statements in possession of General McCook, and they agree in every respect with the testimony taken by a Lieutenant Colonel Tappan, of the First Colorado Cavalry who was at Sand Creek but refused to participate in the slaughter. [17]

Colonel Chivington had no idea that a bitter controversy would arise after he and his men attacked the Indians at Sand Creek. According to the December 22, 1864, edition of the *Rocky Mountain News*, Chivington and the troops were treated like heroes when they first returned to Denver in mid-December. The Colorado legislature passed a resolution expressing the gratitude of the people of the territory to Chivington for his actions. [18]

Many settlers believed the Sand Creek Battle was necessary to teach the Indians that they must come to terms with the reality that they were a conquered people. White men, women, and children could not be stopped from invading their homeland. Pioneers in Central City, Colorado, took the actions at Sand Creek to mean that they had permission to rid the frontier of Indians using any means they saw fit. Some immigrants soaked bread in strychnine and left it on the trail for hungry Indians to find. [19] According to the November 11, 1869, edition of the *Miners Register*, "one hundred men, women and children were killed from eating the poisoned bread." "That is the kind of warfare we approve of," the article continued, "and should be glad to see it introduced here. It is a cheaper peculiarity than to kill them [Indians] with powder and lead." [20]

Satisfied that they had done their best to protect the region from being overrun by warring Indians, members of the cavalry volunteer regiment whose enlistments had ended returned to their homes and families. Colonel Chivington was mustered out of service on January 6, 1865. [21] By then the controversy around Sand Creek had just begun to attract attention. Chivington was being courted by wealthy landowners, merchants, and political leaders as a nominee for Congress. [22] Colorado had yet to be named a state, but hopeful citizens believed it was inevitable and wanted Chivington to be their representative. Those vehemently opposed to the former colonel being involved in any political venture cited his actions at Sand Creek as their reason. [23]

Figure 4.2.   George Bent, a Cheyenne American who chose to live and fight as a Cheyenne warrior, is pictured here with his wife, Magpie. The Denver Public Library, Western History Collection, Z-8878

On January 15, 1865, a formal report was submitted to the war depart-ment by Indian interpreter John S. Smith. After being made fully aware of what had transpired from the men who had served with Chivington, Smith submitted the report requesting that an investigation be conducted. Included in the report were affidavits from the soldiers who witnessed the massacre. When the strongly worded report reached the desk of General Henry Halleck, President Ulysses S. Grant's chief of staff, he quickly agreed that an investigation was necessary. "Colonel Chivington's assault on Sand Creek was upon Indians who had received some encouragement to camp in the vicinity under some erroneous supposition of the com-manding officer at Fort Lyon that he could make a sort of 'city of ref-uge,'" the report read. "However wrong that may have been, it should have been respected and any violation of known arrangements of that sort should be severely rebuked."[24]

Chivington's account of what happened was significantly different from the reports submitted by the officers who served under him. In the official report to his superiors in 1865, Chivington stated:

> My reason for making the attack on the Indian camp was that I be-lieved the Indians in the camp were hostile toward the whites. The idea that they were of the same tribes with those who had murdered many persons and destroyed much valuable property on the Platte and Ar-kansas Rivers during the previous spring, summer, and fall was be-yond doubt.
>
> When a tribe of Indians is at war with the whites it is impossible to determine what party or band of the tribe they are in or the names of the Indian or Indians belonging to the tribe, so at war all are guilty of acts of hostility. The most that can be ascertained is that Indians of the tribe have performed the acts. During the spring, summer and fall of 1864, the Arapaho and Cheyenne Indians, in some instances assisted, or led by the Sioux, Kiowa, Comanche and Arapaho, had committed many acts of hostility. . . . Their rendezvous was on the headwaters of the Republican, probably one hundred miles from where the Indian camp was located. I had every reason to believe that these Indians were directly or indirectly concerned in the outrages which had been committed upon the whites. I had no means of ascertaining what were the names of the Indians who had committed these outrages other than the declaration of the Indians themselves; and the character of the Indians in the western country for truth and veracity, like their lack of respect for the chastity of women who may become prisoners in their

hands is not of that order which is calculated to inspire confidence in what they may say. . . .

With positive orders from Major General Curtis, commanding the department of punishment the Indians should receive, decided my course and resulted in the battle of Sand Creek, which has created such a sensation in Congress through lying reports from interested and malicious parties. [25]

Colonel Chivington did not know exactly how many Indians had been killed in the battle. He estimated that a couple hundred Cheyenne and Arapaho lost their lives at Sand Creek. He was certain there were only a few women and children among the casualties and was emphatic that none had been killed who didn't first attack his troops. "Officers who passed over the field, by my orders, after the battle, for the purpose of ascertaining the number of Indians killed, report that they saw but one woman who had been killed, and one who had hanged herself; I saw no dead children," Chivington noted in his initial report about the battle. "From all I could learn, I arrived at the conclusion that but few women or children had been slain. I am of the opinion that when the attack was made on the Indian camp the greater number of squaws and children made their escape, while the warriors remained to fight my troops." [26]

Contradictory reports from Chivington and the men who participated in the attack prompted not only a military investigation but also a Senate inquiry into the condition of the Indian tribes. [27]

Three days before the House of Representatives passed a bill directing the Committee on the Conduct of War to initiate the investigation, Cheyenne, Arapaho, and Lakota Indians banded together and attacked a way station near Julesburg, Colorado. The Indian army numbered more than one thousand braves, including a well-known Cheyenne warrior named Roman Nose and a Sioux warrior named Crazy Horse. The various Northern Plains tribes combined forces to not only overtake the way station but also raid ranches and stagecoaches up and down the valley of the South Platte River. It was revenge for the slaughter at Sand Creek. Fourteen United States soldiers and four civilians lost their lives at the Battle of Julesburg on January 7, 1865. [28]

After the attack the Indians assembled at a camp near Cherry Creek, Colorado. Mochi was one of the many survivors from the Sand Creek Massacre who had escaped with Black Kettle to the prairie. [29] The forlorn band was grieving the loss of family and friends. Under normal circumstances Mochi would have been able to bury her mother, father, and husband soon after they had been killed. The Cheyenne believed that ghosts might linger near the bodies of the deceased and take their spirit if they weren't buried quickly. This was particularly so with children. Wives would remain at the graves of their husbands, parents would stay at their children's plot, and none could be persuaded to leave for days after their passing. Mourners would cut their hair and gash their heads or legs with a knife, shedding their own blood in remembrance of the loved ones lost.[30]

If Mochi's husband had any property that belonged to him she would have laid him to rest with those items. If the lodge she and her husband had lived in had not been burned to the ground, she would have torn it down herself and given it to others in the community. Mochi would have kept only one blanket for herself and returned to live with her parents. There was no one left from her immediate family to turn to, and, apart from the clothes she wore, she had no personal possessions.[31]

Mochi's despair turned to rage. She joined the warriors who attacked the outpost near Julesburg and vowed to avenge the death of her family. While she and the other Indians planned more raids, a United States military commission prepared to hear testimony about the Sand Creek Massacre from Major Scott Anthony, Indian agent John S. Smith, Colonel Chivington, and many others.[32]

Statements made against Chivington during the investigative hearing were damning. He tried to defend his actions by informing the committee that he had been told by his officers that the Indians along the Sand Creek were hostile. Chivington denied ever being told the Indians were under protection of the government. "I had no reason to believe that Black Kettle and the Indians with him were in good faith at peace with the whites," the colonel assured the interrogators on the case. "The day before the attack Major Scott Anthony told me that these Indians were hostile," Chivington reported. Chivington told investigators he ordered his sentinels to fire on the Indians if they attempted to come into the post and that the sentinel had fired on them for doing so. Chivington anticipated the Indians' attack. Major Samuel G. Colby, a United States Indian agent, told Chivington that he had done everything in his power to make the Indians behave themselves but that "nothing short of sound whipping would bring peace with them."[33]

Figure 4.3.   Major Scott J. Anthony of the First Colorado Cavalry demanded the Indians surrender their weapons and then sent them to set up camp on Sand Creek. The Denver Public Library, Western History Collection, Z-8877

Colonel Chivington, who acted as his own council at the hearing, was adamant that he did not approve, authorize, or even know of any mutilations of Indian bodies at Sand Creek and requested any and all evidence to the contrary be presented to him. He would not accept the word of army officers who testified to the atrocities seen at Sand Creek. Chivington believed those men were pro-Indian and traitors to their country. "Damn any man who sympathizes with Indians," the colonel recalled telling his troops. "I have come to kill Indians, and believe it is right and honorable to use any means under God's heaven to kill Indians."[34]

Cheyenne Indians usually rested during the winter months, but what happened at Sand Creek and the trail surrounding it changed their way of life. They declared war on the United States, and the Dog Soldiers specifically wanted to make Chivington answer for his actions.[35]

When word that serious problems loomed on the frontier reached President Abraham Lincoln, he ordered more than seven thousand troops to travel west to help bring order. Mochi, along with hundreds of other bitter Indians, promised to fight to the death against "white man's" idea of peace.[36]

5

THE MISSING

A Cheyenne storyteller sat cross-legged in front of an open fire in Black Kettle's lodge near Cherry Creek, Colorado. Black Kettle and several warriors and elders were spread out across the room watching the smoke rise from the fire and disappear through a hole in the top of the tepee into the night sky. Mochi was with them, seated behind the old men, listening to them talk and to the sounds beyond the lodge.[1]

Black Kettle filled a pipe and lit it. He then pointed the pipe stem to the sky, then to the ground, and then to the four directions: north, south, east, and west. Before handing the pipe to the storyteller sitting on his left, he called upon the "Listeners-Above-the-Ground, Listeners-Under-the-Ground, and the Spirits Who Live in the Four Parts of the Earth." After saying a prayer, the storyteller took the pipe from Black Kettle, smoked it, and began to talk. He told the story of what had happened at Sand Creek, of the brave dead that lay under the cold, dark sky the evening after the massacre. He told about the white army that slaughtered women and children and of the blood spilled that would forever be remembered.[2]

Tales generally told by the storyteller were his alone to share. Cheyenne history and sacred beliefs were kept alive by storytellers and could not be told by others. If the storyteller wanted he could give the story away in the same way he might give away a blanket or some other gift. Black Kettle's lodge was filled with Indians who had no use for such a gift. They had their own stories about the Sand Creek Massacre. Tales of what they witnessed would be passed on by them from generation to generation. It would haunt their dreams and drive them, and their own stories of the horror would never cease.[3]

Mochi, along with the others on hand to hear what the storyteller had to share, said nothing while he was speaking. It was believed that any noise or moving about while the sacred stories were being relayed would bring great misfortune upon the camp. When the ceremony ended Mochi walked out of the lodge with the others. For the time being her home was with her cousins. When she wasn't helping with meals and caring for children she was learning the ways of the Dog Soldiers and preparing for more attacks on white settlers.[4] Colonel Chivington's attack on Sand Creek was meant to destroy the Indians' will to fight, but it didn't work. According to George Bent, who became a Dog Soldier after the massacre, many warriors refused to accept the United States government's plan for the native people and banded together to retaliate.[5]

A number of Cheyenne, including Black Kettle, refused to take up arms against the United States, however. They separated themselves from those braves who chose to stand their ground. Black Kettle didn't want any more bloodshed. Bands of Southern Arapaho, Kiowa, Comanche, and Cheyenne moved south of the Arkansas River, eventually making peace with the white man and signing a treaty promising to end the conflict.[6]

In late 1865, more than one hundred Cheyenne Dog Soldiers and six hundred Sioux and Arapaho warriors attacked the Valley Stage Station, Moore's American Ranch, and Harlow's Ranch, all near Julesburg. They drove off herds of cattle belonging to settlers and hundreds of cavalry horses and left in their wake burned homes, stores, and corrals. They shot and killed soldiers and captured and kidnapped women.[7] The reputation of the Dog Soldiers for being particularly ruthless and savage spread from one army post to another. Descriptions of how they dressed, the way they painted their faces, and their revenge raids made members of wagon train parties heading west fearful for their lives.[8]

In the August 9, 1886, edition of the *Galveston Daily News*, one witness recalled:

> I was at the Julesburg massacre in January and at Moore's Ranch when more than a hundred soldiers and forty-two citizens from both places were made to bite the dust. These Dog Soldiers wore long belts made of tanned skins and they painted themselves red, black and yellow. I was wounded in three places in my first tangle with them. I was shot in my side and through my leg and my head was cut open. The Indians

pillaged Julesburg and the storehouse at the ranch. While they were pillaging in Julesburg we crossed the river on the ice to get to safety. The Indians engaged in the massacre were Sioux and Cheyenne under the control of Bad Wound. They rode up around us on three sides and poured a dreadful fire upon us at short range.[9]

Dog Soldiers participated in a second raid on Julesburg on February 2, 1865.[10] According to George Bent's account of the attack, a small band of Indians first tried to lure the soldiers out of their stockade. The plan was to get the troops in the open, overtake them, and ride into the un-guarded stage station. The soldiers did not fall for the Indians' ploy. The warriors regrouped and descended on the stockade together. George Bent noted in his memoirs that the Dog Soldiers rode past eighteen graves of men killed in the first attack on Julesburg. Six hundred Indians fought their way to the warehouse at the stage station and broke into the store onsite.[11] Mochi was one of the Cheyenne who helped gather the food and other provisions together and herded the horses away from the war-torn stockade. When there was nothing left to plunder, the Indians set fire to the buildings.[12]

Mochi and the other Indians left Julesburg and headed across the Great Divide between the South Platte and North Platte Rivers. Telegraph poles lining the path they followed were destroyed. They were either burned or chopped down, and the wires were cut and carried away or tangled up and tossed into the brush. Regiments of cavalry troops from Mud Springs, Nebraska, and Camp Mitchell, Wyoming, rallied and pur-sued the Indians, but the warriors would not allow themselves to be easily driven from the valley.[13] Because of the Sand Creek Massacre, raid upon raid was carried out on soldiers and settlers from February to October 1865. Many warriors and white men lost their lives. Like other Dog Soldiers, Mochi would have taken part in the killing and the ritual mutila-tion of her enemies.[14]

Somewhere in the midst of the fighting and retreating and fighting again, Mochi met a warrior named Mihuh-heuimup or Medicine Water. He had lost his wife at Sand Creek and was raising his young daughter Tahnea alone. Medicine Water and Mochi shared a strong desire to elimi-nate the white man from their homeland and to preserve the traditions and lifestyles of the Cheyenne people. If not for the Treaty of the Little Arkansas, Mochi and Medicine Water might not have considered mar-riage. They would have continued their attacks on United States troops and buffalo hunters until one or the other were killed, but a remission in the weekly fighting gave them the chance to rest and consider life beyond the battle.[15]

The United States government grew weary and annoyed fighting the Indians. It wanted peace. It wanted settlers to travel on the Santa Fe Trail unchallenged, and it wanted the Indians to be relegated to a limited section of earth. In exchange the major Plains Indian tribes demanded to be allowed to hunt in the region and asked for reparations for the Sand Creek Massacre. The parties met at the mouth of the Little Arkansas River to discuss the contract. The terms were agreed upon and the treaty between government commissioners and representatives of the Cheyenne, Arapaho, and associated tribes was signed on October 15, 1865.[16]

Mochi, Medicine Water, and several other Indians did not believe the government would honor the treaty they signed. They were right. In less than two weeks' time the treaty was broken. White buffalo hunters poached on the ground which the treaty had made sacred to the Indians. Mochi, along with other warriors, again took up arms against the white man. The fact that she was now a new mother did not stop her from going to war. Mochi and Medicine Water's newborn daughter and Tahnea stayed at the lodge with the other women and children whenever there was a battle to be fought.[17]

Another cease-fire between the Northern Plains Indians and United States government came about in October 1867 with another treaty signed on the banks of the Medicine Lodge Creek in southern Kansas.* The Indians were to be provided food, clothing, and farming equipment, schools and churches, a resident agent, doctors, and other such services.[18]

In turn the Indians agreed not to molest whites, interfere with travel, hamper railroad construction, or raid any forts in the western country. According to the October 31, 1867, edition of the *New Albany Daily Leader*, the Cheyenne Indians were hesitant to enter into any other agreements with the United States government. The Arapaho, Comanche, and Kiowa assembled together to meet with the Indian Affairs Commission, but the Cheyenne were slow to arrive on the scene. According to the article:

> Dispatches from Medicine Lodge Creek say a treaty with a portion of the hostile Indians may be all government officials can hope for. All the tribes are to be sent to the same reservation in the Oklahoma Territory. They are to receive $5,000 per annum as well as clothing,

etc. All the tribes here except the Cheyenne held a council on the 28th and agreed to renew friendly relations with the United States and return any stolen horses.

The Cheyenne have not arrived yet, and some suspect bad motive on their part while others think all will come out all right. They claim they have not yet finished their medicine ceremonies and ask two days longer time. The commission has already waited thirteen days on this tribe and is now tired. They will remain until Monday the 30th when they will leave if the Cheyenne are not here. [19]

The Cheyenne arrived at the peace accord on January 27, 1867. The Dog Soldiers were at the head of the peace party. Black Kettle and the other members of the tribe followed closely behind them. [20] Before signing the treaty, Black Kettle reiterated a statement he had made to the commission at the Little Arkansas River in 1865. "I have always been friendly to the whites, but since the killing of my people at Sand Creek I find it hard to trust a white man," he told the commissioners. To further emphasize his point he had his wife stand before the group and show the commission the injuries she sustained at the Sand Creek Massacre. Soldiers had shot her several times during the battle. The nine bullet wounds she received were evidence of the cruelty visited upon the Indians at Sand Creek. The commissioners were sympathetic with Black Kettle's position and after much discussion encouraged him that signing the peace treaty was in the best interests of the Indian people. [21]

Congress was slow in ratifying the treaty. It would be more than a year before some of its provisions were carried out. The Plains Indians were angered by the delay. They interpreted Congress's actions as further proof of the white man's bad faith. War parties from some of the tribes banded together again. Mochi and the Dog Soldiers were eager to join in the fight. [22] Men such as George Bird Grinnell, a student of Native American life who spent time with the Indian tribes during the Plains Wars, never had faith in the Medicine Lodge Treaty. According to his recollections in the book *The Fighting Cheyenne*, the offer of a "few presents and the signing of treaties by a few chiefs would not appease the Indians whose livelihood, the buffalo, was being destroyed and driven away." The clash of conflicting interests was inevitable. [23]

Dog Soldiers didn't agree with Black Kettle's decision to sign the Medicine Lodge Treaty. They disagreed with the idea that the only peace they would find would be in the treaties made with the whites. Mochi and the other Dog Soldiers reminded the chief that the treaty signed in September 1864, before the Sand Creek Massacre, had not brought peace. He was also reminded of the Little Arkansas pact. Among the many things the government promised the Indians were supplies and peace in exchange for any white prisoners held hostage. The government did not deliver on its promises.[24]

While waiting for the best time to take action against the Unites States government, Mochi and Medicine Water concentrated on raising their children. The couple would eventually have two more daughters of their own. Mochi and her adopted daughter Tahnea were extremely close. The little girl idolized Mochi, never wanting to leave her side. Stories of their profound bond were told for generations.[25]

By the winter of 1868, the Cheyenne were camped at the bank of the Washita River in the Oklahoma Territory. The region was hospitable to the Indians. There was plenty of water and firewood and an abundance of grass for their horses to eat. A bitter, cold northern wind scattered snow over the camp, but its 250 inhabitants were safe inside their lodges with fires burning to keep them warm. For a time all was quiet.[26]

On the morning of November 27, 1868, the stillness in the camp was broken by rifle shots and cavalrymen that descended upon the lodges from all directions, and the unfamiliar strains of "Garry Owen" blasted through the early dawn. When the sun made its full appearance Black Kettle got his first look at the chaos in and around the camp. Riding at the lead of the main column was General George Custer. Confused tribesmen scurried in every direction; each sought refuge from the stinging, death-dealing fire of the soldiers' guns. High-pitched screams of tiny children mingled with the dying groans of old men. Brave Indian youths sacrificed their lives so others might have a few minutes longer on earth. Grief-stricken mothers clutched the limp bodies of children as they, too, turned the white snow scarlet with their blood.

Black Kettle's wife ran into the battle leading her husband's horse behind her. When she reached the chief he attempted to mount the horse. In mid-air, a well-aimed bullet found its mark and Black Kettle fell across the back of the horse, dead. His wife leaped upon the animal behind the chief. She never made it to the river and the scant protection she sought there. Both bodies fell from the frightened animal and slid into the snow.[27]

Figure 5.1.   This photograph, taken circa 1875, is said to be of Medicine Water and Mochi upon arriving at the prison where they would be held for eight years. State Archives of Florida, *Florida Memory*

Some military leaders such as General Custer argued that the Cheyenne, and in particular Black Kettle and his warriors, were outside the fixed boundaries that had been designated in the treaty. The Indians understood that the treaty gave them the right to hunt on any lands south of the Arkansas River as long as the buffalo in the area were in large numbers. The misunderstanding was lethal. General Custer ordered troops to burn the entire village, shoot most of the tribes' nine hundred ponies, and take any surviving women and children hostage.

Cavalry soldiers were injured in the dawn raid when the Indians fought back against their attackers. According to the June 29, 1868, edition of the *Indianapolis Journal*, Mochi and Medicine Water could have been with the warriors that battled with Custer's men.

A victim of Indian vengeance has returned to his home in upstate New York. His name is Delos G. Sandberton and he lost his scalp at the battle of Washita. He has been an inmate at Laramie Hospital since that event, and was discharged about ten days ago. He has allowed the curious to examine his head, and gave the following account of his experience.

"I was in the infantry. Custer had command of the troops," Sandberton shared. "There was quite a force of cavalry with us, but they were about a mile in the rear when we first discovered the reds. Some of the troops had been sent around so as to attack from the other side. Just in the grey of the morning, the firing commenced on both sides, and we had it all our own way for a few minutes, the cursed snakes being much confused and not knowing what was up. At length they rallied, and we could hear Black Kettle shouting and ordering. The vermin got into holes and behind rocks—anywhere they could find a place, and all began to fight back with a will. We fired whenever we could see a top-knot. When it was fully daylight we all gave a big yell and charged right down into the camp. The lodges were all standing and there were lots of Indians in them.

"As we ran through the alleys, a big red jumped out at me from behind a tent and before I could shorten up enough to run him through with a bayonet, a squaw dressed as a Dog Soldier grabbed me around the legs and twisted me down.

"The camp was full of men fighting and everyone seemed to be yelling as loudly as he could. When I fell, I went over backwards dropping my guns and I had just got part way up again, the squaw yanking me by the hair, when the Indians grabbed my gun and struck me around the neck. The blow stunned me and the squaw kept screaming and pulling my hair out by the handful. I heard some of our boys shouting close by. The Indian stepped one foot on my chest and with his hand gathered up the hair near the crown of my head. He wasn't very tender about it, but jerked my head this way and that, like Satan. My eyes were partially opened and I could see the beadwork and trimming on his leggings. Suddenly I felt the awful biting, cutting of flesh go around my head, and then it seemed to me just as if my whole head had just been jerked clean off. I never felt such pain in my life. If the boys killed the viper and his squaw they didn't get back my scalp; perhaps it got lost in the snow."[28]

Cheyenne history notes that Mochi fought valiantly during the Battle at Washita, but, while defending her home and children from the soldiers,

she was separated from her daughter, Tahnea. The five-year-old girl panicked when she saw the people in the village running for cover. Tahnea
fell in with the others racing about and became disoriented by the screams
and gunfire. She ran toward the river behind several women and children
who plunged themselves into the icy water. Unable to swim, Tahnea
stopped at the edge of the water to consider what to do next. A cavalry
sharpshooter saw her, took aim, and fired.[29]

When the fighting subsided Mochi began the desperate search for her
daughter. Some Indians reported they saw Tahnea struck by a bullet and
die. Others said she was only wounded and had stumbled back toward the
camp. They speculated that she might have been killed in the blaze that
consumed the lodges. Mochi sifted through the ashes of the bonfire but
couldn't find any trace of her child. In despair, she resolved Tahnea had
fallen into the water and drowned and that her body was lying at the
bottom of the Washita River.[30]

*The Medicine Lodge Treaty consisted of three treaties in total. The first of the three was a
treaty made with the Kiowa and Comanche Indians, the second was with the Plains Apache,
Kiowa, and Comanche Indians, the third was negotiated with the Arapaho and Cheyenne
Indians.

6

LESSONS FROM YELLOW-HAIRED WOMAN

Two days short of the fourth anniversary of the Sand Creek Massacre, General George Armstrong Custer and his troops attacked a sleeping Indian encampment near the Washita River. The Cheyenne who were not killed were taken hostage. An expert from General Custer's report described the scene of the event as "gruesome." "Men stabbed through with shotgun barrels, Cheyenne women and children clubbed to death," he noted.[1] Custer claimed that "squaws and children had been slain in the excitement and confusion of the first charge."[2]

For many mourning Indians such as Mochi, the ruthless attack was not dissimilar to the Sand Creek Massacre. Several articles in East Coast newspapers defended the army's decision to raid the Indian camp because the Indians continued to attack white settlements and military outposts. According to the December 29, 1868, edition of the *Daily Rocky Mountain News*, Custer was "led to the hostile camp by following the trail of a war party that were returning from raids west and south of Fort Riley." The article continued:

They had fresh scalps and four white men in their possession. One was that of a military express rider who was butchered and horribly mutilated but a few days before between Fort Dodge and Fort Larned. The mail he was carrying was found in the conquered camp. The contents of rifled mails, effects from plundered settlements, and the green and reeking scalps of murdered citizens were also found in the captured camp. There were those who cried "friendly Indians" and "another

Sand Creek Massacre" lustily at first, but it quickly dwindled to the faintest whisper. Thank God the military, civilization, and the cause of the frontier settler are victorious this time.[3]

For the Cheyenne who escaped the actions of Custer and his men the invasion was unjustified. Mochi and other women from the tribe wrapped the bodies of the warriors in blankets and bound them with ropes in order for them to be moved from the area and buried. More than one hundred women, children, and braves were slain. Several acres of dead ponies lay among the slaughtered Indians, unconcealed. Once the grim task of caring for the deceased tribesmen was done, Mochi and the other Dog Soldiers left the area. She and the other warriors went in the opposite direction of the Indians who decided to relocate to the reservations the United States government had assigned to them in the Medicine Lodge Treaty of 1867.[4]

While the Cheyenne were either moving on to reservations or establishing other camps in the plains and planning counterattacks against the military, Custer's report on the Battle of Washita was making the rounds. This report, addressed to General Philip Sheridan, head of the Department of the Missouri, a command echelon of the United States, read:

> On the morning of the 26th, this command, comprising eleven troops of the Seventh Cavalry, struck the trail of an Indian war party. My men charged the village, and reached the lodge before the Indians were aware of our presence. The moment the charge was ordered, the band struck up "Garry Owen," and, with cheers that strongly reminded me of scenes during the war, every trooper led by his officer, rushed toward the village.
>
> The Indians were caught napping for once, and the warriors rushed from their lodges and posted themselves behind trees and in deep ravines, from which they began their most determined defense. The lodges and all their contents were in our possession within a few minutes after the charge was ordered, but the real fighting, which was rarely, if ever, equaled in Indian warfare, began when attempting to clear out or kill the warriors posted in ravines and underbrush; charge after charge was made, and most gallantly too, but the Indians had resolved to sell their lives as dearly as possible. After a desperate conflict of several hours, our efforts were crowned with the most complete and gratifying success.

The entire village, numbering forty-seven lodges of Black Kettle's band of Cheyenne, two lodges of Arapaho, and two lodges of Sioux, fifty-one lodges in all, under command of their principal chief Black Kettle, fell into our hands. By a strict and careful examination, after the battle, the following figures give some of the fruits of our victory.

The Indians left on the ground, and in our possession, the bodies of 103 of their warriors, including Black Kettle himself, whose scalp is now in the possession of one of our Osage guides. We captured, in good condition, 875 horses, ponies and mules. Two-hundred forty-one saddles, some of very fine and costly workmanship; 523 buffalo robes, 210 axes, 140 hatchets, 35 revolvers, 47 rifles, 535 pounds of powder, 1,050 pounds of lead, 4,000 arrows, 90 bullet-molds, 35 bows and quivers, 12 shields, 300 pounds of bullets, 775 lariats, 940 buckskin saddle-bags, 470 blankets, 93 coats, 700 pounds of tobacco. In addition, we captured all their winter supply of dried buffalo meat, all their meal, flour and other provisions, and, in fact, everything they possessed, even driving the warriors from the village with little or no clothing. We destroyed everything of value to the Indians, and have now in our possession, as prisoners of war, fifty-three squaws, and their children. Among the prisoners are the survivors of Black Kettle's and the family of Little Rock. We also secured two white children held captive by the Indians. One white woman, who was in their possession, was murdered by her captors the moment we attacked. A white boy held captive, about ten years old, when about to be secured was brutally murdered by a squaw, who ripped out his entrails with a knife.[5]

As Mochi and the other members of the tribe put distance between themselves and the horrific setting at the Washita River, the sound of the Central Pacific and Union Pacific Railroads encroaching upon the land could be heard. The cry of the engine whistle not only signified impending doom for the buffalo, whose great numbers had been diminished with the flood of white settlers on the frontier, but also meant the end of the Indians. Mochi was unwilling to go along quietly with what the United States government insisted was the fate of all Indians in the face of progress. Heartsick and angry over the loss of her daughter, Mochi followed after Medicine Water and the band of braves who were set on making the white intruders pay for their atrocities.[6]

Shortly after the Battle of Washita, Medicine Water was made a leader in the Bowstring Society. The Bowstring Society was a warrior military sect. They were exceptional marksmen with a bow and arrow. They were tenacious, cunning, and, because of what they had witnessed at the hands of the United States cavalry, ruthless and unforgiving.[7]

Mochi was devoted to the society and its cause. She patterned her actions after another female warrior of fierce renown, Ehyophsta or Yellow-Haired Woman. The thirty-seven-year-old Cheyenne woman had fought in major battles and proven she could be as violent and menacing as her male counterparts during a skirmish with the Shoshone Indians. In 1869, Ehyophsta pursued a Shoshone warrior to a spot between the Colorado-Texas border where she and her tribe had been fighting. During their clash she managed to stab and scalp the Indian she was battling. Mochi desired to be just as courageous.[8]

Mochi and Medicine Water were still lamenting the loss of Tahnea when the five-year-old girl was returned to the Bowstring camp in June 1869. A member of another tribe of Cheyenne Indians led by a chief named Little Robe found Tahnea hidden in the banks of the Washita River. She had been shot and was severely injured, the bullet having hit her in the hip. The parent and child reunion was a heartfelt occasion but the drive to confront the United States Army over what had been done did not subside. Tahnea had been left crippled and her life changed forever.[9]

Newspapers such as the *New York Tribune*, *New York Times*, *New York Post*, *Philadelphia Press*, and *Chicago Tribune* criticized the events that took place at the Washita River and compared General George Custer to Colonel John Chivington. According to Chivington's biography, he believed Custer's actions were justified. In his opinion the "government's lack of uniform policy, and its alternating between extreme severity and foolish sentimentality in dealing with the savages, only accentuated and prolonged the conflict."[10]

By the time the Battle of Washita took place, Colonel Chivington had long been removed from the military. The multiple hearings to review his actions at Sand Creek resulted in his castigation and a ruling that would keep Chivington from ever serving in the army again.[11]

Concerned that the controversy surrounding the massacre would create problems within the church if he were assigned a flock to minister, Chivington opted to keep his name on the inactive list. He believed he was too bitter to preach. He was angry about what he deemed were "unjustified and vicious attacks" on him by the military and the public.[12]

6.1.   The Seventh U.S. Cavalry charging Black Kettle's village at daylight during the Battle of Washita. T
Library, Western History Collection, X-33802

Although he was never again assigned as the pastor of any local congregation, he was still connected with the church as a member and would serve as an agent of the Nebraska Conference Church Extension Society. John moved to Nebraska after the incident at Sand Creek and invested in a freighting business. The business was not without its setbacks; the wagons were frequently attacked by the Indians and entire shipments of goods were either stolen or destroyed.[13]

From time to time supporters of Chivington would request he come and speak to various civic organizations about his views on the Plains Indians, the military, and government leaders. In October 1866, he was asked to address some of his admirers at Council Bluff, Iowa. According to a report in the November 1, 1866, edition of the *Sullivan Democrat*, Chivington's statements were incendiary and biting. "If we go to heaven and any Democrat dare intrude there, we will kick him out," he told the crowd. "If we go to hell, we will heap fire and brimstone on them. Yes, I would stand on the battlements of heaven and kick Democrats into hell; and, if I go to hell, I will pour a cauldron of red hot iron down upon them."

"This language would sound strange coming from the mouth of a true Christian," the *Sullivan Democrat* reporter added, "but coming from Chivington whose sole military exploit was the coldblooded massacre of the Sand Creek Indian women and children, it is just what might be looked for."[14] In addition to business losses, Chivington's personal life suffered as well. On June 26, 1866, his only son, Thomas, drowned in the North Platte River while crossing with a load of government freight. His body was not recovered until March of 1867, and funeral services were held soon after. Two months after Chivington laid his son to rest, his granddaughter fell off a steamship that was traveling along the Missouri River and drowned. In August of that same year, Chivington's wife of twenty-eight years died from a gastric ailment.[15]

News of Colonel Chivington's losses would no doubt have been well received by members of the Bowstring Society but wouldn't have served as just punishment for the massacre at Sand Creek. The Indians were dedicated to fighting back against the injustice done. Between May and June 1869, the Cheyenne Dog Soldiers, along with a band of Oglala Sioux, raided a number of white settlements in Nebraska and Kansas. Many homesteaders and their wives and children were killed and women were kidnapped and raped.[16]

On July 11, 1869, a United States military campaign devoted to the Nebraska frontier pursued the Indians northwest toward the Platte River near Sterling, Colorado. The cavalry anticipated that the Indians would cross the river and then escape into the sand hills, but they didn't. They were so confident they could overcome the troops that they made camp. A battle ensued and the Indians lost. Among those killed was the leader of the Dog Soldiers, Tall Bull. Surviving Dog Soldiers fled the area but would regroup later and be led to war again, this time with Medicine Water and Mochi in charge.[17]

In the early 1870s, the Bowstring Society and remnants of the beleaguered Dog Soldiers fought government surveyors encroaching on unsettled Indian Territory. The Cheyenne uprooted stakes the surveyors had driven into the earth and drove the workers off the Indians' hunting grounds. However, more surveyors came. On March 19, 1873, Mochi, Medicine Water, and more than twenty of their warriors decided to make an example of a land surveying crew camped along the Cimarron River in Oklahoma.[18]

The April 8, 1873, edition of the *Janesville Gazette* was just one of many newspapers that reported on the murder of the workers.

> The facts in this gruesome tale are appalling. It seems that Downing and Barrett, government contractors, have their surveyors divided into several parties, and the head compassman of one of these parties sent out a young Mr. Deming, whose father is well known as the proprietor of the hotel in Arkansas City, with two chainmen and a flagman, whose names are not given, a mile and a half or two miles from camp to correct a line run the day previous. Staying longer than they should have done, the party went out to look for them and shortly made an appalling discovery.
>
> Upon the sandy plain were certain marks that the ground had been thrown over something lately and took but little work to reveal underneath it the bodies of their four comrades. Eddie M. Deming, the nineteen year old captain of the crew had no idea there was any trouble with the Indians when he set out with his party to complete the work they'd been hired to do. He expected to get the work done by noon.[19]

In a letter to the editors at the *Janesville Gazette*, Hugh F. Richards, one of the members of the survey team, wrote:

At about 11 a.m. he sent one of the cornermen to camp. He got to it all right. When he left the party they had about three miles to meander down the left bank of the Cimarron River. Eddie and his party failed to get in that night, but as no one anticipated they were in any danger we did not suspect there would be any trouble with the Natives although they were very thick through the section. As they did not get in by noon on the 20th we got very worried. A party was sent to look for them.

They struck their trail on the riverbank and followed it until they arrived at the town line where Eddie had closed and finished his work. They there found a great many Indian tracks. A band of some forty or fifty warriors had crossed the river below the town line. From the closing point the tracks turned upstream, in the direction of the camp. We suppose the Indians acted friendly and allowed Eddie and his men to start toward camp, then, as soon as they had their back turned, shot and killed them and buried them where they fell.

When the boys found the mounds of sand with tracks ending at them, they tore away some of the sand and recognized the body of Eddie M. Deming. The bodies of the men were found stripped of all their clothing and possessions. Three were untouched by wild animals and were not scalped, but the bodies were decomposing. Eddie had been scalped and his flesh eaten by wild animals; only the bones remained. As there were hundreds of Indians within a mile, they did not wait any longer, but started toward camp getting in (a distance of about ten miles) in about one and half hours. We stood guard all night, but were not attacked and rolled out for headquarters in Arkansas City the next morning about an hour before daylight.

The murdered men are Eddie M. Deming, son of Mr. A. M. Deming, proprietor of the City hotel in this city; Daniel Short, of Lawrence, Kansas, Charles A. Davis of Cream Ridge, near Chillicothe, Missouri, and R. Pool, a young Englishman of Lawrence, but he has no relatives in America.

There is still a party of thirteen men in danger and a provision train belonging to Captain E. A. Darling, surveyor and contractor. About thirty of us start out today to bring in the other party and train if possible and recover the dead bodies of our murdered comrades. If the parties who report that the Indians are disposed to be quiet on the frontier would take a trip out among them for a little while they would soon change their minds. I am certain that they are anything but peaceably inclined.

>One band of Indians has declared their intent to fight all summer
>long and will commence as soon as grass is high enough for feed. [20]

The actions of Medicine Water and his band of Indians was a declaration of the Indians' determination to continue fighting. Different tribal groups decided to join forces with the Cheyenne to rid the plains of white intruders. The next raid took place in the Texas Panhandle at an abandoned trading fort called Adobe Wall. Trappers and buffalo hunters had made the post their temporary headquarters, and the Indians in the territory resented it. Plans were made to attack Adobe Wall on the morning of June 27, 1874. [21]

More than two hundred warriors raided the fort where thirty well-armed soldiers had taken refuge. The fighting was long and well sustained. Marksmen in front and behind the gates at Adobe Wall shot many Indians in the storming party. According to the August 8, 1874, edition of the *Anglo American Times*, "Seventeen Cheyenne and six Comanche were killed on the spot and a large number of both tribes mortally wounded." The Indians eventually retreated. Not a single settler defending the post was shot or killed in the exchange. [22]

The costly defeat prompted warriors from tribes riding with Medicine Water and Mochi to surrender to United States Indian agents and to agree to move onto reservations. Mochi rejected the idea. It was well known among the Cheyenne that Indians could die of starvation at a reservation if the government decided not to feed them. Mochi preferred to die in battle avenging her family lost at Sand Creek. [23]

Although their numbers had been depleted, the Bowstring Society pressed on. The senseless slaughter of her parents and first husband and the permanent injury sustained by her daughter after being shot at Washita were always at the forefront of Mochi's thoughts. She was out for blood and the full force of that drive would be visited on an immigrant family camping along the Smoky Hill River on Kansas land the Cheyenne considered to be rightfully theirs. [24]

7

SAVAGE AND CRUEL

Ten years after the Sand Creek Massacre, animosity between the Comanche, Cheyenne, Arapaho, Kiowa, Pawnee, and Sioux Indians, and white settlers was still raging. The band of renegade Indians crisscrossing territory from Colorado to Kansas struck out at anyone who threatened to deprive its members of their traditional way of life. The Bowstring Society, led by Medicine Water and his warrior wife Mochi, did not have the braves or weapons needed to lead successful raids on significant army posts or stage stops, so it concentrated its efforts on wagon and freight trains, land survey crews, and army scouting parties. [1]

In July 1874, pioneers and explorers happened onto a gruesome scene near Buffalo Springs Station, a relay station in Oklahoma for the United States mail. Three freight wagons had been overturned and set on fire by Cheyenne Indians. The burned corpses lying on the ground next to the wreckage prompted travelers to reconsider heading west for fear of being killed. The short battle between the Cheyenne and a stubborn Irish freighter named Patrick Hennessy had been witnessed by a mail carrier and a station attendant as they hurried south along the Chisholm Trail. Patrick had chosen to ignore warnings about the warring Indians and pressed on with two other drivers, George Fant and Thomas Caloway. [2]

According to historian and author T. G. McGee, within five minutes of the freight driver's leaving the station multiple gunshots were heard by the mail carrier and the station attendant. The two men raced to the top of a bluff just in time to see the Indian raiders attacking the drivers. "George and Thomas were shot down a short distance from Pat," the mail carrier and station attendant told soldiers later. "Pat was killed and tied to the two wheels on one side of the wagon and then a torch was applied to the wagon. All three wagons were thought to be carrying grain. One who passed two days later stated that the grain was still smoldering in a heap over poor Pat's charred remains, and his limbs were almost burned from his sturdy body as he lay spread there between the two charred wheels."[3]

When the settlers living and working at Buffalo Springs Station viewed the site where the men had been killed, they were horrified. According to the mail carrier's account of the incident in the *Chronicles of Oklahoma*, no one was willing to go near Patrick Hennessy to bury his remains. "He was lying on the east side of the Chisolm Trail. . . . The position of the burning body gave evidence that the man, still alive, had been tied to the two wheels by the chain traces of his own wagon."[4]

Cheyenne Indian agent John Miles noted in his report to the government that Patrick Hennessy had struggled greatly to break loose from the ties that bound him. "His ankles and feet were all that could be used to recognize the fallen freight driver," Miles wrote. "Much of the sugar, coffee, oats and corn were hauled away by the Indians. All of the men were horribly mutilated and scalped." All were eventually buried where they died.[5]

Ida Dyer, the wife of one of the Indian agents in the territory, recalled in her reminisces printed in 1896 the terrifying thoughts travelers had as they journeyed by the graves. "We felt the wickedness of the Indians' power in his own country," Ida wrote, "and shivered and shuddered as we passed on."[6]

The reign of terror that gripped the Indian Territory continued long after Patrick Hennessy and his fellow freighters met their demise. In late August 1874, an unsuspecting survey crew lost their lives in southwestern Kansas near a well-known frontier landmark called Lone Tree.[7]

Captain Oliver Francis Short led the party of twenty-two government engineers out of Lawrence, Kansas, on July 29, 1874. They were to cover 920 miles marking the boundaries of the land occupied and belonging to the Plains Indians. Among those traveling and working with Captain Short was his fourteen-year-old son Daniel Truman Short, Captain Cutler and his sixteen-year-old son Harry Cutler, James Shaw and his eighteen-year-old son J. Allen Shaw, Clem Duncan, William Richard Duncan, Frank Blacklidge, twenty-two-year-old Harry C. Jones, and eighteen-year-old John H. Keuchler. On August 15, 1874, Captain Short and his team made camp east of Lone Tree, and the following day he wrote his wife to let her know that all was well. He shared with her that water had been located for the crew and the oxen and that there was an abundance of stones available to use as cornerstone markers. [8]

Captain Short and the other engineers discussed what to do if irate Indians saw them and threatened to attack. It was agreed that they would set fire to the buffalo grass around them. The decision was later rescinded in favor of preserving the grass for their oxen. On Sunday, August 23, Captain Short led the crew in a brief Bible study and in singing hymns. The rest of the day was spent doing such tasks as laundry, checking survey equipment, and tending to the livestock. The following morning buffalo hunters stopped by the camp and shared coffee and biscuits with the men. Captain Short sent the letters to his wife with the hunters who were headed to Dodge City, and the survey crew prepared themselves for a long day of work. [9]

Captain Short sent eleven men from the expedition north to survey. Short took five men with him and traveled south. He left his son Harry behind to tend to the camp duties. The entire team was scheduled to meet back at the camp on Monday, August 31. Less than two days after the survey crews took to the field, disaster set in. The men working north of the camp had no idea Captain Short and his team had met with trouble until his wagon was found abandoned near a creek far from where the captain and his group were supposed to be. [10]

The eleven-member team was suspicious, and they immediately armed themselves. They approached the wagon cautiously, guns ready to fire at anything that moved. It wasn't until they reached the empty vehicle that they saw the bodies of Captain Short and his entire team lying face down in the dirt, dead. The Cheyenne had killed the luckless surveyors and laid their victims in a row. The oxen used to pull the wagons had been killed as well, and the hind quarters of the animals had been cut off. According to the May 1932 edition of the *Kansas Historical Quarterly*, Captain Short, his son, and Harry Jones had been scalped, and the others had their heads crushed. A compass was hammered into the head of one of the men and the pockets of all the men had been turned inside out. [11]

Upon further investigation by the eleven men who found their slain cohorts, the first point of attack was located. Captain Short and his team were eight miles from the camp they had established a few days prior. The Indians had surrounded the survey group and Captain Short and his men had run toward the wagon for cover. There were twenty-eight bullets found in the water barrel attached to the side of the wagon. The ground around the scene was littered with cartridge shells and survey equipment. The September 6, 1874, edition of the *Atchinson Globe* reported that on Thursday, August 27, 1874, a party of hunters arrived at the geographical survey crew's camp and informed the group that "they had been chased by a body of twenty-five Indians the day or two previous to the attack on Short's party but succeeded in getting away from them."[12]

Once the Indians were out of sight the hunters backtracked and examined the Indians' camp. Some of Captain Short's papers were found, along with parts of his surveyor's chain. Mochi confessed after her arrest that the camp belonged to Medicine Water. The captain and the other slain men were buried near the lone cottonwood tree on the plains where they died. Their bodies were later removed and laid to rest at their family cemeteries. Captain Short's wife organized the effort to bring the surveyors home. Mrs. Short went on to file a claim against the State of Kansas for her loss and was later awarded $5,000.[13]

Stories of how white settlers continued to suffer the wrath of Medicine Water's band traveled from outpost to outpost. Panic set in among pioneers, and many refused to venture any farther than Independence, Missouri, until the government could assure their safety. Colonel Nelson Miles was ordered by commanders of the United States Army to lead an aggressive campaign against the Cheyenne and capture the Bowstring Society chief, his wife, and the 276 other Indians fighting with them.[14]

Not everyone agreed with the government's approach. Military officers such as Lieutenant Charles Gatewood, politicians such as Ulysses S. Grant, and members of the clergy believed the actions of the Indians were justified to an extent. They did not advocate the wholesale torture and murder of white men, women, and children, but argued that the Indians' actions had been prompted by the United States government's treatment of them. "The name of Cheyenne is representative to many persons of all that is savage and cruel. There is nothing which soothes conscience like the abuse of those whom we have wronged," wrote Bishop Henry Whipple in the February 22, 1879, edition of the Greencastle, Indiana, newspaper the *Greencastle Star*. "The Cheyenne were among the friendliest of the Indians of the plains. They were a brave, noble type of red men."[15]

After gold was discovered in California, the United States made a treaty for the right of way across the Indian country in which the Cheyenne joined. "For this right the government agreed to pay $50,000 annually," Bishop Whipple further explained about the plight of the Indian in the *Greencastle Star* article:

> No white man was to settle on the Indians' land. This treaty was faithfully observed by the Indians. Emigrants crossed the plains in safety, singly, in companies, in ox-trains, and on foot. Once the cry of gold was heard throughout the land the Indians were forgotten. It is then many Cheyenne became unfriendly. Cities were laid out and lots sold upon Indian lands.
>
> The press of immigration drove the buffalo and the Indians south. The Indians' annuity payment ceased. The Indians were sad and depressed, but they kept the peace. Black Kettle, their chief, was our friend. He knew the power of the whites and dreaded war.
>
> One day a body of troops was seen crossing the prairie. Black Kettle took a United States flag in his hands and his two brothers' white flags in his hands and hoisted them as a sign of friendship. White Antelope, one of these brothers, had just returned from an errand of mercy. He had gone at Black Kettle's request one hundred miles to warn the mail coach that the Kiowa were on the war path. The goodwill messengers were fired upon by the troops, and the brothers were both killed. Black Kettle went to his tepee where there were three white men in United States uniforms and said to them, "I believe you are spies; it shall never be said that a man ate Black Kettle's bread and came to harm in his tent. Go to your people before the fight begins."
>
> Black Kettle gathered his little band and fought so bravely that he saved a part of his people. Between two hundred and three hundred men, women, and children were butchered. Babes were scalped in their mothers' arms, women with children were ripped and their unborn children taken from their mothers' wombs and the scalps of babies taken as trophies of victory. Scenes took place that day which were so horrible that the language cannot conceive of such barbarity. Thus ends the first chapter of our dealing with the Cheyenne. Black Kettle, who loved his people with blind devotion, who knew the power of the whites and dreaded the certain doom of Indian war, still pleaded for peace. For this he was near being deposed of his chieftanship by the Indians. The Sand Creek Massacre changed the course of the future between the Indians and white man.
>
> From November 1864 forward neither Northern or Southern Cheyenne have been admirers of the white men. More treaties were made with these noble people and all were broken. The Cheyenne refused to

make another treaty with the United States. Their bitter experience had taught them. I need not tell the history of the deaths on the plains.

For whatever blunders and excesses were made by the government, the real sufferers are the innocent people of the border. . . . I need not go on. I envy no man's head or heart that reads the last eight years of the Cheyenne history and does not feel pity for this hunted, outlawed people. I tremble for my country when I remember that God is just. [16]

Colonel Chivington disagreed with Bishop Whipple and maintained that the United States Army needed to "enact God's justice." According to an interview Chivington's third wife, Isabella, did with historian Fred Martin in 1902, the colonel never deviated from the notion that "Indians who had committed depredations should be killed." The war department's investigation into the Sand Creek Massacre ended with no charges being brought against Chivington or his troops. The military did turn its back on Chivington and his name became synonymous with torture and murder. Colonel Chivington dismissed any disparaging comments about his actions, standing by his decision and insisting to all who would listen that he was justified. "[The Indians] are guilty of robbery, arson, murder, rape and fiendish torture," he continued to tell family, friends, and supporters. "I believe it right and honorable to use any means under God's heaven to kill Indians who kill and torture women and children." [17]

From January 1865 to July 1869, Chivington crisscrossed the western territory in search of a place to settle, grieve the loss of his military career, mourn the deaths of his wife and son, and avoid any further backlash because of Sand Creek. He returned to Nebraska in the spring of 1868 to attend a religious conference. From there he traveled to Chicago, where he visited with his son Thomas's widow, Sarah. The two became romantically involved and were married on May 13, 1869. [18] Sarah's parents were distraught over their daughter's relationship with her former father-in-law and made their feelings known in the June 13, 1868, edition of the *Petersburg Index*. "We, the undersigned, take this method to inform the public that the criminal act of John M. Chivington in marrying our daughter was unknown to us and a thing we very much regret," Sarah's father, John Lull, announced in the short article. "Had the facts been made known to me of the intentions some measures would have been taken to prevent the consummation of so vile and unnatural an outrage," he continued. "Even if violent measures were necessary I would have stopped it. Hoping this may be a sufficient explanation for what has occurred, we remain, John and Almira Lull." [19]

The Chivingtons divorced less than two years after they exchanged vows. Chivington abandoned his bride and fled to Canada without providing monetary support for her. "He left me with nothing," Sarah explained to a pension examiner in Washington, D.C., via letter. "And I had no desire to live with a criminal." Sarah and John Chivington's divorce was finalized on October 25, 1871. [20]

By mid-1873, Chivington had met and married Isabella. She was a forty-four-year-old widow of a Union soldier. The pair lived on a farm in Clinton County, Ohio, then relocated to the town of Blanchester. It was there Chivington traded in his plow for a newspaper called *The Press*. For several years Chivington had been on the editorial staff of publications such as the *Christian Advocate of St. Louis* and the *Nebraska Methodist Quarterly*. He made time for the job no matter what else he was doing to support himself. [21]

Throughout the Red River War, the name given to the military campaign the United States launched to remove the Comanche, Kiowa, Southern Cheyenne, and Arapaho Indian tribes to reservations, Chivington expressed his opinion about the Indians' continual uprisings in the West. "As I said at the onset of this war," Chivington wrote in the March 12, 1875, edition of *The Press*, echoing a statement he had made in 1864, "the Cheyenne will have to be roundly whipped or completely wiped out before they will be quiet. I should have been more vigilant. Damn any man who sympathizes with the Indians." [22]

The frustration Chivington felt over the Indians' behavior manifested itself in his marriage. He was physically abusive toward Isabella. She had him arrested not only for beating her but also for stealing money from her. Isabella appeared in court with a black eye and a bruised face, and the judge was ready to sentence Chivington to several years in prison for his actions. At the last minute Isabella decided to drop all charges and forgive her husband. He promised to pay the court costs, return his wife's money to her, and never raise a hand against her again. According to an article in the August 15, 1881, edition of the *Clinton County Democrat*, "Chivington's debt to the court has yet to be paid." [23]

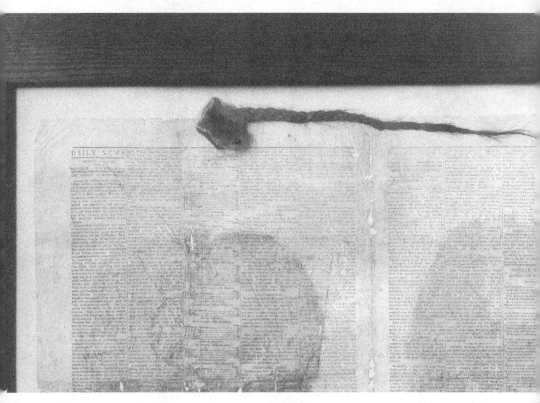

Figure 7.1.   This Indian scalp was taken by one of Colonel Chivington's troops at the Sand Creek Massacre.
aintain that the soldiers decorated their belts and saddles with these items. The Denver Public Library, W
ollection, X-32078

Isabella felt sorry for her husband and the battle that raged within his soul. "He was a tormented man," Isabella told historian Fred Martin in 1902. "He was unable to secure peace in Colorado, and I got in the way of the torment."[24]

It took Chivington and the events at Sand Creek to set in motion the war that had been brewing between the United States government and the Indians since the Homestead Act was passed in 1862. The act granted individual settlers 160 acres of land each—in land already occupied by Indians.[25]

Nothing Mochi or the other members of the Bowstring Society had done reversed the move Congress had made or changed the fact that settlers continued to pour onto the plains undeterred. No sooner had the Bowstring Society dealt with one survey crew encroaching upon their land than another one followed. Not only was the Cheyenne war party contending with various geographical expeditions, but Colonel Nelson Miles and his troops were closing in on them, as well.[26]

The United States Army caught up with Medicine Water, Mochi, and the other warriors on August 31, 1874, at the Washita River's headwaters and engaged them in a running fight. The Indians managed to get away, but not before losing one of their own in the skirmish. They rallied again after a second encounter with Colonel Miles, which resulted in the loss of a guide named Mule Smoke who had led the Indians out of danger. Determined never to surrender, the Cheyenne renegades regrouped and rode on to attack one last time. Their next raid would be among the most shocking of all in the Red River War.[27]

8

MOCHI

The sun had not quite risen over the vast Kansas plains when John German heard a sound that tempted him from his work packing his family's belongings into their wagon. He surveyed the campsite with a careful eye. His wife Lydia and their seven children were each going about their morning chores and preparing to continue their journey to Colorado. The Germans were from the Blue Ridge region of Georgia and had spent the summer of 1874 traveling west. They planned to reach their new home before winter.[1]

John and Lydia's oldest children, twenty-year-old Rebecca Jane and nineteen-year-old Stephen, were tending to the livestock in a field not far from the family campsite. For a brief moment all seemed as it should be; then, suddenly, a small herd of antelope darted across the trail, panicked. Several shots rang out, and the antelope scattered in different directions. Another shot fired and a bullet smacked John in the chest, and he fell in a heap on the ground. Lydia ran toward her husband. Nineteen members of the Bowstring Society rode hard and fast into the German family's camp, whooping and yelling. Lydia continued running. A Cheyenne Indian on horseback chased her down and thrust a tomahawk into her back.[2]

Rebecca Jane grabbed a nearby ax and attempted to fight off the warriors as they rode toward her. She managed to hit one of her attackers in the shoulder before she was knocked unconscious with the butt of a gun, raped, and killed.[3]

Fifteen-year-old Joanna crawled to an empty, wooden box in the back of the wagon and waited, too terrified to move. She watched helplessly as her sisters—seventeen-year-old Catherine, twelve-year-old Sophia, seven-year-old Julia, and five-year-old Adelaide—stood huddled together, flanked on all sides by the Indians. Joanna's long curls dancing in the hostile breeze caught the attention of one of the Indians, and he rushed over to the girl with his rifle in hand. He shot her, and she collapsed in the dirt, dead. Her sisters looked on in rapt terror as the Indian set his gun aside and scalped his victim.[4]

Mochi, who had participated in the raid, scanned the bodies of the German family before she dismounted her ride. With an ax in hand she walked to John's lifeless frame, stopped and studied the blood gushing from his wounds. In a ghastly tribute to her own family who were slaughtered at Sand Creek, Mochi drove her ax into John's head and then did the same to Lydia. According to Catherine German's reminiscences, the "Indians then took what they wanted from our wagon. In a short time my once happy family life was forever ended."[5] Catherine later recalled:

It only took a few moments to dash down upon us. With such surprise we could have done nothing, even if we had had good firearms. We may have been watched during the night.[6]

The Indians took us four frightened sisters, our six head of cattle, other booty and started in the direction whence they had come. Later, I was told they set fire to the wagon and burned what they did not want; as I do not remember seeing a blaze I think this was done after we were out of sight. I have no idea how far we rode until we came to where they had left their saddles and other traps. They always rode bareback when they made a raid. After making a short stop to get their belongings, the Indians traveled onward and soon crossed a stream of clear water. Oh, how I wished for a drink, but my captors gave no heed to my gestures.[7]

After a while they stopped and killed our cattle, roasted the meat, sang and made merry over the terrible deed of that morning. Indians offered us meat, but we were so terrified and heartsick that we could not eat. We four, sad captives huddled together terribly frightened. We were so shocked and stunned that we could scarcely realize what had happened. I could not think, and only saw over and over the dead bodies of my parents, sister and brother. I heard again the awful outcries of the Indians and their victims.[8]

The morning of the day we were captured was clear and bright, but about noon a rain storm burst upon us. This was the first rain since we had left Elgin, Kansas. How it lightning and thundered! After the first hard shower, it rained slowly all afternoon and evening. We had no shelter. The little girls were still so frightened that they kept very quiet. Doubtless, our recent tragic experience had taught silence. I noticed the change in Adelaide for she had been always afraid of strangers and had manifested her fear by crying and now she seemed awed into silence. As we rain-soaked, pitiful children huddled together, we tried to comfort one another in this our great distress and grief.[9]

The Cheyenne war party traveled south with their captives in tow. On the second day of the journey back toward the panhandle of Indian Territory, the warriors stopped to divide their prisoners among them. The two youngest girls were taken by the only other woman riding with the Bowstring Society and her husband. A young brave claimed Sophia for himself, and Mochi and Medicine Water took Catherine. "Then they bridled up the horses," Julia remembered months after the ordeal, "and put sister [Addie] in front of one young buck and me in front [of] another on horseback. We were jolted until our necks got stiff."[10]

According to the December 12, 1874, edition of the *Neosho Valley Register*, Catherine and Sophia were raped multiple times by Medicine Water and the other Indian tribesmen. On one occasion Catherine was stripped, painted, and tied to a horse by Mochi. Then she was "put on the prairie" as the Cheyenne called this accepted cultural practice. Several young men in the camp rode Catherine down and violated her. The *Neosho Valley Register* noted that "white women were considered as guilty as men who came to seize Indian lands and buffalo and they were treated in the way women of ill repute were treated."[11]

Mochi was said to have been crueler to the teenagers after such attacks. "I felt a great dislike for that large squaw," Catherine remembered in her account of the horrific event and of Mochi. "From the first she proved to be a hardhearted, brutal, cruel savage."[12] She continued:

Sometimes we were given roasted pieces of meat because a squaw would see we could not eat the half-raw meat that the Indians enjoyed. The large squaw seemed delighted to see us tortured or frightened. Once when I was roasting a piece of liver over the camp fire, Big Squaw snatched it from the stick which held it and ate it just before I had finished cooking it.

Another day, a buck tried to make us eat raw meat and because we would not do so, she threw firebrands at us and would not let me come near to cook the meat. Big Squaw and the other Redskins often tried to frighten me by saying they were going to kill me. Sometimes I heard the threat and felt the muzzle of the gun against my back but I stood very still for I felt that death would be better than living a miserable life with them. I was despondent and did not care really what happened to me.

A few more tricks the Indians played on me. . . . Once they tried to make me believe that I was to be drowned. Early one frosty morning the large Indian who was with Big Squaw and who captured me made me go to the near-by creek and a crowd of mischief-loving fellows followed us. They doubtless expected to see some fun. There was a deep pool on our side of the creek, so my captor pushed me down the bank into the cold, deep water. Instead of struggling to get out, as they expected, I swam to the opposite side of the pool and walked out. How surprised they were! There were shouts of laughter for the joke was on the buck who pushed me into the pool and he had to wade a narrowed part of the stream to get me. No other attempt was made to drown me since they learned that I could swim. How I shivered! I had no other clothes so those had to be worn until they dried.

Sometimes for their supper they enjoyed a skunk roasted whole: hunger induced me to eat a piece of the liver. When they killed a prairie chicken, Big Squaw threw it away instead of allowing me to cook it. I would have been grateful for such a delicious morsel.

Another encounter with Big Squaw came one day when I became warm and let my blanket fall to the ground. Several squaws carried axes for the purpose of felling trees. At length I decided to get my blanket, which lay behind the large squaw who was trimming off the low branches of a tree. She did not see me, and as I stooped to pick up my blanket, she drew her ax back to chop into the tree trunk, the blunt end of the ax cut a gash in the top of my head—not a very deep one— but, though slight, it bled quite freely. [13]

Exactly how long and how far the Indians rode hauling their prisoners behind them is unclear. Prior to their arrival at the Cheyenne's main camp sometime after September 24, 1874, Catherine noticed that her mother and sister's scalps had been divided into five pieces. She surmised that it was to represent the number of persons they had killed in her family. [14]

By the time the first snow fell in 1874, the Indian band that Catherine was with had ridden into New Mexico. She recounted in her memoirs years later:

Figure 8.1.   Sophia German was twelve years old when she was beaten and raped by her captors. Mochi was one of those Sophia saw drive an ax into her father's head. Item #781, Call #B German Family 2 Kansas State Historical Society

Figure 8.2.   Catherine German was the oldest of the German sisters captured and tortured by the Cheyenne Indians in 1874. Item #772, Call #B German Family 1 Kansas State Historical Society

Figure 8.3.   Adelaide and Julia German. Adelaide was five years old when she witnessed the murder of her parents. She and Julia were held hostage together for several months. K/978.1/IS2 Kansas State Historical Society

The wind had ruthlessly stripped the trees of joy, comfort, and the real necessities of life, but hope and faith were left to me. I had occasion to recall the words of an invalid lady with whom I stayed for a while in Sparta, Tennessee. She had said to me one day, "The Indians out West sometimes take little girls." I had carelessly replied, "If they get me, they will let me go." At that time, August 1874, I entertained no thought of captivity by the savages, but now when such was a reality, I courageously longed for deliverance, or that some way of escape might be possible. While these aborigines of America were not fearing pursuers they seemed to have a good time visiting and eating. I believe that they could eat more food, or, if necessary, they could fast longer than any other human being I have ever known. [15]

Catherine was handed over to a Cheyenne Indian couple while Mochi and the other members of the Bowstring Society continued their raids on settlers in the northern plains. She survived almost three months not knowing the fate of the three sisters from whom she had been separated. Finally, in early December Catherine caught sight of Sophia at the edge of a canyon in New Mexico, where she had been living with her Indian caretakers. Catherine recounted several years later:

She was sitting on a horse, bareheaded but otherwise well wrapped up. She had become so tanned by exposure to the sun that her complexion resembled that of an Indian and I did not recognize her from a distance.

What a joyful meeting that was. We cried and cried for joy, but that did not please the Indians who seemed to think that tears meant weakness, so they said we must be separated. However, we were together all that evening and part of the next day. A short time after we really began to visit, Sophia said, "Have you seen Julia and Addie?" I was astonished and it was several seconds before I could speak in reply. I was wondering if she was in her right mind. At last I answered, "I dreamed last night that I saw them both, alive and well, but I have not seen them, nor do I ever expect to see them again."

Sophia replied, "They were alive a month or six weeks ago, for I saw them." Then she told me how it happened that she saw [our] sisters. An Indian came to Sophia one morning just after sunrise and motioned her to follow him. She was afraid to go, so he took her by the arm and pulled her along and released her only after they were in a lodge. The Indian wanted her to see the white captive children recently brought to camp. Sophia saw a little figure lying there on some blankets. Soon she recognized her seven-year-old sister Julia who was so weak and dizzy that she could scarcely sit up. Julia told Sophia that when the Indians first left them they motioned for them to follow, which she and Addie did for a while, but the Indians were soon out of sight. At last they wandered along a creek and found a place where soldiers had once camped. Here the children found grains of corn scattered about where the horses and mules had been fed; crackers and other scraps of food were there. These, Julia and Addie ate, and when this food was gone, they gathered the ripe plums, hackberries and wild ripe grapes from the trees and vines. They also ate tender stems and roots of wild onions and other harmless plants. [16]

According to the December 12, 1874, edition of the *Neosho Valley Register*, by December 8, 1874, the United States cavalry was closing in on the Cheyenne raiding parties. An army scouting party from Fort Wallace had discovered the bodies of the German family several days after they had been slain. A family Bible was found at the scene and the dead were identified. The scouts reasoned that the missing children had been abducted. When news of what had happened to the German family reached people at outposts and settlements they demanded the girls be found. Soldiers in the panhandle were ordered to spare no effort in their search. [17]

Mochi was aware that the military was pursuing her and the other tormented Cheyenne in her company. Indian hunters and trackers kept a vigil on their itinerant camp and alerted the tribe whenever soldiers were in the vicinity. Dressed as a typical warrior and carrying a hunting rifle, tomahawk, and butcher knife, Mochi proudly followed Medicine Water from the campsite to the open plains, always running and hiding from tenacious troops. Mochi never wavered in her desire for vengeance. She daily recalled the details of how her family was killed and how quickly she lost everything dear to her. [18]

From the moment Colonel Miles and the infantry units in his command that rode with him during the autumn of 1874 were tasked with locating the German girls, the Cheyenne were continually on the move to avoid being captured. Miles divided his troops into three columns, and they swept over the plains in an attempt to drive Mochi, Medicine Water, and their allies into the troops stationed along the border of Texas and Indian Territory. At times food was lacking for the Cheyenne and their horses. Game was scarce, buffalo in particular, and the time that was needed to hunt for anything to eat was spent keeping ahead of the army. [19]

Figure 8.4.   General Nelson Miles was a United States soldier who served in the Civil War and Indian War. He led troops on a mission to rescue the four sisters taken by Mochi and the other warring Cheyenne. Library of Congress LC-DIG-Stereo-1S02855

In the account of her captivity, Catherine German noted:

> The severity of the winter was one of the best allies the soldiers could have had in subjugating the Indians. The ponies and horses were dying by the hundreds from starvation. The Indians were forced to eat the flesh of those starved animals, thus saving their own lives. I became very hungry for bread, fruits or vegetables. Even grains of corn would have been relished.
>
> One night I went to bed hungry, and dreamed that I crawled along a lightly traveled wagon road and searched for grains of corn. Later I dreamed that I saw little sisters, Julia and Addie, walking toward me. Then I awoke to regret that it was only a dream. [20]

On January 15, 1875, the chief of the tribe that cared for Catherine called her to his lodge and handed her a note written by General Nelson Miles. The note informed her that Julia and Addie had been found alive. A column led by Lieutenant Frank Baldwin had located the village where the two girls were living. The soldiers fought the Cheyenne in a skirmish that lasted more than four hours. During the battle the Indian women and children managed to flee the area with the tribe's herd of ponies. The cavalry eventually overtook the Cheyenne village. Julia German was hiding under a buffalo robe when the soldiers found her. Addie was racing in and out of the lodges looking for her sister. She was so weak from hunger that she fell down a number of times trying to get to Julia. [21]

The Indians who had Catherine and Sophia decided to leave their campsite. The girls were ordered to help pack the tribe's belongings and they all set out in a northeasterly direction. According to Catherine, knowing her sisters were alive gave her and Sophia the "courage to endure hardships." [22]

Five days after Catherine received news about Julia and Addie a second note was delivered to the camp. An English-speaking Kiowa Indian had been sent by the United States Army to track the Cheyenne and present the message to Catherine. The military feared the girls might be killed if they tried to overtake the Indians en masse and believed the Kiowa stood a better chance of reaching the captured teenager. Catherine recalled some time later:

> From beneath his blanket he drew a package and handed it to me. I unwrapped it at once and was delighted to find a photograph of dear

little sisters, Julia and Addie. General Nelson Miles had sent the pictures to me. . . . On the back of the picture was pasted a message, "To the Misses Germaine [*sic*]: Your little sisters are well, and in the hands of friends. Do not be discouraged. Every effort is being made for your welfare." I wanted to show the picture to Sophia, so that she might share my joy, but the Kiowa wished the return of it at once.

You may be sure I found Sophia as soon as possible. She was in a lodge not far from the chief. These guardians seemed to be taking special care of their captive. Sister was much pleased to know that I had seen the picture of our sisters and to hear the encouraging message written on the back of it. The cheerful thought that efforts were being made for our benefit by the Major General of the United States Army helped us to take courage and to hope that soon release would come. [23]

Colonel Miles was determined to rescue Catherine and Sophia. Throughout the bitter winter months of 1874–1875, he and his troops relentlessly pursued the warring Plains tribes. Little by little, the bands surrendered, and some were forthcoming about where the girls could be found. Military dispatches were sent to reason with Indians reluctant to admit defeat. They were promised safe passage to the reservation only if Catherine and Sophia were alive and well. [24]

It was almost evening on March 1, 1875, when the two oldest German girls were led onto the Cheyenne Indian reservation. The military had crushed the Indians' ability to resist. Slowly they moved to army garrisons to surrender. The band of Indians holding Catherine and Sophia captive were the last to give in. Mochi and Medicine Water were a part of that band. In her memoirs of her time as a Cheyenne captive, Catherine noted:

Soldiers from the military headquarters came to meet us and for one-half mile they lined the road on both sides. They waved their caps and shouted welcome to us. I cannot tell you how very, very glad we were. We cried and cried for joy as we rode into safety among our people. "Safe at last! Safe at last!" were the words that repeated themselves in my mind. Our hearts were full to overflowing, of gratitude, both to God and to the brave men who had rescued us.

Sophia and I were taken first to the Mission school where the white ladies greeted and welcomed us. How sympathetic, good and kind they were to us poor orphan girls. We must have looked very forlorn to them; our hair unkempt, our bodies thin; and our faces and hands roughened and weather beaten.[25]

My first inquiries were for the welfare of our two small sisters, Julia and Addie. I learned that they were in good care at the home of Mrs. Patrick Corney in Fort Leavenworth, Kansas. We needed to rest and live under quiet conditions. The newspapers reported that the two older German girls had been surrendered by the Indians and were living at the Mission school. Many interested travelers stopped to see us. These visitors increased in numbers until the military officers considered it best to station a guard at the door of the school. For a fortnight, all inquirers who wished to see us were asked to go to headquarters and obtain a pass in order to be admitted by the guard. Although we were very thin, we were not especially weak; our strenuous life with the Indians had kept our muscles hard and firm. Sophia's weight was sixty pounds and mine only eighty. Sophia was twelve years and six months, and twenty days after we arrived at the Cheyenne Mission school I celebrated my eighteenth birthday.[26]

The German girls weren't the only ones suffering from malnutrition. The majority of the Cheyenne Indians were half-starved as well. The buffalo was all but gone, having been hunted by white men to near extinction. At thirty-four, Mochi's face was weathered and gaunt, and her eyes were cold and desperate. No one seemed to recall the agony that began for her at Sand Creek as she rode past the troops behind her husband.[27]

Mochi wrestled with the military guards who pulled her from her horse and corralled her with the other members of the Bowstring Society that had surrendered. Some of the Cheyenne were led to quarters where they could settle into their new living environment comfortably. Mochi and Medicine Water were placed in irons and taken to the guardhouse.[28]

9

LIFE AT FORT MARION

Mochi watched the activity in the camp through the iron bars on the window of a cell. The residents of the Oklahoma Territory garrison were busy with their regular duties: stacking cords of wood, practicing marching drills, and cleaning their weapons. Some of the soldiers were collecting money and clothing for the German girls. Mochi had heard from the Indian prisoners who spoke English that the girls' suffering "appealed to every sentiment of sympathy in the warm hearts and gallant men who rescued them." A total of $185 had been collected and would be presented to Catherine and Sophia before they were to be sent to join their younger sisters in Kansas.[1]

Shortly after Mochi arrived at the Darlington Cheyenne Arapaho Agency near El Reno, Oklahoma, she had stood with the other renegade Indians to be identified by the German girls as the ones who attacked their family. Both Catherine and Sophia pointed to Mochi and, holding back the tears, told the onlookers what she had personally done. "She is the one who chopped my mother's head open with an ax," Sophia announced. Mochi did not deny it. Like the other Cheyenne who witnessed their loved ones slaughtered at Sand Creek, she considered her actions no more disturbing than those of the soldiers.[2]

According to Catherine German's memoirs, Mochi did not seem bothered at all when she saw Catherine and Sophia for the first time after being rescued. Medicine Water, on the other hand, "turned ashy color and seemed much frightened," she wrote. "I recognized him at once as the husband of Big Squaw and one who had been active in the raiding band responsible for the death of our folks. The Colonel had the guards line up all the warriors in the camp as if for roll call and he led Sophia and me down that long line of Indians. I recognized but two of the seventeen Indians who were in the raiding band on September 11, 1874. Besides the arrested buck, I found his wife Big Squaw, and I was not sorry to see them take her prisoner, for as you know, she was never kind to us captive girls. She seemed to enjoy seeing the bucks tease or torment us."[3]

Catherine and Sophia described the many ways Mochi had been abusive. The Indian woman said nothing; there was no one present to offer a defense for her or the other seventy-five Cheyenne warriors charged with murder. One of the officers who oversaw the prisoners noted in the records he kept that "Mochi was so distinguished for fiend-like fierceness and atrocity that it was not deemed safe to leave her on the plains. She was a fine looking Indian woman but was as mean as they come."[4]

On April 6, 1875, Mochi, Medicine Water, and the other Cheyenne prisoners were paraded before the Darlington Agency blacksmith to be fitted with manacles. Once the metal bands were welded and in place around the Indians' hands and feet, a length of chain was fastened to the irons. The captives' movements were severely hampered. Those who struggled against being restrained were held in place at the point of a gun. The accused had not been tried in a court or been formally sentenced by a judge or jury. The United States military had been ordered to transport the detainees to a location in Florida, but the Indians did not fully understand what was happening.[5]

Cheyenne women watching the scene sang songs in an attempt to persuade the prisoners to break free and to fight and die rather than be led away to an unknown land to merely exist. An Indian named Black Horse defied the soldiers and broke away from the group before he was shackled. Members of the tribe cheered his heroics and urged him on. Black Horse managed to leap onto a horse and ride toward the wooden gate surrounding the camp. Army troops leveled their guns at the Indian and a barrage of bullets struck him in the head and chest. He was dead when he fell off his mount and hit the ground. A stunned silence hung in the air for a brief moment before processing the prisoners resumed.[6]

Humiliated and confused, the captives were loaded onto an eastbound train headed to a region the Indians would find inhospitable and unforgiving. Grey Beard, a Bowstring Society warrior who had fought with Mochi and Medicine Water, was determined never to reach the destination white leaders decided was fitting for all Indian renegades. In late May 1875, he jumped from the train as it was leaving a station in northern Texas. The May 26, 1875, edition of the Greencastle, Indiana, newspaper *The Press* described the daring attempt to escape. "Grey Beard, the most troublesome of the Indian prisoners leapt from the locomotive while it was running twenty-five miles an hour," the report read. "The train stopped and the soldiers found him secreted in the bushes one hundred yards from the tracks. The troops fired on the Indian and a ball passed through his body above the waist. He expired as the train was leaving Sanderson about two hours after being shot."[7]

Another Bowstring Society member attempted suicide while en route to the Florida prison. According to the May 23, 1875, edition of the Athens, Tennessee, newspaper the *Athens Post*, "the Indian known as Lone Bear managed to get hold of a knife, with which he stabbed two soldiers and then himself," the article noted. "It is reported that the soldiers are not seriously hurt. On the arrival of the train in the city of Nashville, Lone Bear was taken off and laid on the platform, wrapped in his blanket, and is supposed to be in dying condition."[8]

Lone Bear survived and was later transferred to the prison at Fort Marion. Being confined drove him mad, and three months after being locked away soldiers were urged to remove him from the premises. The August 5, 1875, edition of the *Greencastle Banner* reported that the "Indian became insane" and that "an application had been made to have him sent to a government insane asylum near New York."[9]

Mochi was lean and frail when she arrived at the gates of the Florida prison at the end of May 1875. She and Medicine Water were processed into the facility at the same time. Their records described their physical condition and the crimes for which they were being held:

> Medicine Water: Mi-huh-yeu-i-mup. Warrior. Age 40. Wt. 139 lbs. Ht. 5 ft. 7 ¼ in. Arrested at Cheyenne Agency, Indian Territory, March 5, 1875. Charge #1, willful and deliberate murder. Did kill or assist in killing a party of surveyors, white men, consisting of Captain Oliver F. Short and his son F.D. Short, James Shaw and his son, J. Allen Shaw and J.H. Renchler, residents of Lawrence, Kansas. Also Henry C. Jones. Charge #2, abduction, illegal detention, kidnapping. Did carry off or assist in carrying off Catherine, Sophia, Julianne, and Mary German, aged respectively, 17, 13, 7, and 5 ½ years. Held the first two as captives from September 11, 1874, until March 1, 1875.

Figure 9.1. Interior of the Fort Marion prison where the Indian inmates would congregate daily. State A
Florida, *Florida Memory*

> Mochi: Woman. Age 34. Wt. 138 lbs. Ht. 5 ft. 6 ¾ in. Arrested at
> Cheyenne Agency, Indian Territory, March 5, 1875. Put an ax in head
> of Germain [sic] girl's father.[10]

Mochi and Medicine Water were led to a small tent that was to be their home for as long as they were interned at the prison. The Indians were served three meals a day which consisted of bacon, beef or tripe, potatoes, beans, molasses, rice, soup, and tropical fruit. Each was issued coffee, sugar, salt and pepper, and soap.[11]

Every other day, armed guards escorted the prisoners to the beach to supervise the Indians as they bathed. Everything the Indians did, from eating to sleeping and all activities in between, was supervised. Mochi and many other Indians on site had difficulty adjusting to the constant surveillance and their surroundings. Some followed Lone Bear's example and tried to kill themselves. They cut their throats, starved themselves, or hurled themselves off the stone walls of the prison onto the rocks lining the sea. The dead were given non-Indian burials. Their bodies were placed in pine boxes along with all their belongings and buried in a graveyard in the southeast corner of the grounds.[12]

Illness was a continual problem for the Indians. Heat exhaustion and gastro-intestinal ailments were the most common complaints. It wasn't until the inmates were ordered to clean the algae-stained walls and ceilings of their cells and re-canvas their moldy tents that the Indians' physical health somewhat improved. Nothing could be done to help those suffering from severe homesickness, however, until a spokesman for the captives petitioned the federal government to allow their families living on reservations to come and stay with them. On July 22, 1875, Secretary of War William Belknap agreed to the request with the stipulation that there would be "one wife to one Indian and no children over the age of twelve."[13]

Cheyenne leaders at the Darlington Agency were unenthusiastic about the idea of sending for tribespeople from their homeland. They did not trust the government to see their people to Florida safely and respectfully and had serious doubts that anyone would be returned to the reservation when the prisoners' time had reached an end. Cheyenne chiefs ultimately refused the removal of any more tribal members.[14] On August 9, 1875, President Grant revoked the order to send the families.[15]

Mochi's long, dark hair was cut short, as was the hair of all the Indians in her husband's band. Their native clothing was replaced with uniforms: forage caps, blouses, trousers, knit shirts, and shoes. They were made to learn to read and speak English.[16] The transition from life on the plains to life in prison was impossible for Bowstring Society members like Big Moccasin, who killed himself in early November 1875. The Indian warrior was suffering from a deadly fever accompanied with nausea and vomiting. He initially refused treatment but was later made to take medicine the doctor at the facility prescribed. He showed signs of improvement, but again his fever spiked and he had trouble breathing. The physician examined him and discovered that Big Moccasin was suffering from "incontinence of urine" brought on from a swelling in the genitalia. The Indian had tied his genitalia together with a leather cord, and, as a result, the organ had swollen and urine was not allowed to pass. The Indian was given a stimulant to revive his health, but it didn't work. He died on November 4, 1875, and the cause of death was listed as suicide.[17]

Military officers in charge of the conditions at the prison continually tried to make the Indians adapt to the non-Indian world. Many inmates committed to learning all they could from the various classes offered at the facility. Whether it was math, reading, or agricultural courses, there were Indians who wanted to be educated. According to records maintained by Lieutenant Richard Pratt, a superintendent at the prison, former Dog Soldier Making Medicine believed education was "necessary for the social and economic improvement of his people."[18]

Making Medicine is reported to have told Lieutenant Pratt:

> I have led a bad life on the plains, wandering around living in a house made of skins. I have now learned something about the Great Spirit's road and want to learn more. We want Washington to give us our wives and children, our fathers and mothers, and send us somewhere we can settle down and live like a white man. Washington has lots of good ground lying around loose, give us some of it and let us learn to make things grow. We want to farm the ground. We want a house and pigs and chickens and cows. We feel happy to have learned so much that we can teach our children.[19]

Not everyone felt as Making Medicine did. Some Indians, including Mochi, resisted attempts to change. They refused to renounce their tribal ways of life and conform to the idea that the Indians should seek education and employment among those Americans who preferred them to be gone.[20]

Superintendent Pratt's efforts to "civilize the Indians" were a curiosity to many prominent educators, and some visited the prison to see the effectiveness of the program. Among those who came to Fort Marion was Dr. M. B. Anderson, the president of Rochester University, Presbyterian pastor and teacher J. D. Wells of Brooklyn, New York, and author Harriet Beecher Stowe.[21] All were generally impressed with what author K. Johnstone referred to as "Pratt's ability to transform savages into citizens."[22]

According to the January 25, 1877, edition of the *Athens Messenger*, Stowe observed the Indians dressed in United States uniforms as "neat, compact, trim, with well-brushed boots, and nicely kept clothing and books in their hands." She remarked that they were a "strong, thoughtful sensible race. There wasn't a listless face or wandering eye in the whole class." Stowe attended church with the Indians. She listened intently when the congregation knelt and bowed their heads to pray. Although she could not understand the words they were saying, she believed "a succession of moans communicated the wrongs, the cruelties, the injustice which had followed these children, driving them to wrong and cruelty in return."[23]

Stowe also toured the "great kitchen" of the prison, and it was there she saw Mochi, the "woman warrior" she'd heard about. Mochi was busy making a "great caldron of savory soup." "She stood over a stove stirring the boiling pot of meat and vegetables until they were ready to be served. She then set out dishes with meat and bread." Stowe remarked that the meal was a "pleasanter style of diet," but it was obvious from Mochi's stoic expression that she preferred "eating the hearts of enemies." She was defiant and resented being made to do work deemed suitable for women prisoners to do; she still saw herself as a warrior. Mochi also resented influential visitors who came to the prison to study the tribes.[24]

Learning to read gave the Indians the ability to learn the government's plans regarding their future. The October 30, 1875, edition of the *Indianapolis Journal* contained an article about the Committee on Indian Affairs and its mission for the Indians. "Our objective is to take the subject out of the dark, undisciplined, superstitious life into a civilized and Christian culture," the report noted. "It is work that must look well into the natural mind and heart and see clearly what we desire them to be and to believe."[25]

In addition to reading about the United States' plans for the Native Americans, the Indians read about military officers they had encountered when they were living on the plains. Newspapers made available to them by merchants and tourists from the nearby town of St. Augustine contained information about Colonel Nelson Miles, General George Custer, and Colonel John Chivington. Many Indians were unhappy that Chivington, as well as the other men who fought alongside him at Sand Creek, were free men.[26]

Chivington's life off the battlefield was as controversial as when he served with the First Colorado Volunteers. Not only had he been physically abusive to his wives but on two occasions had also been suspected of burning down the homes where he and his family lived in order to collect the insurance on the property. In spite of his dubious and immoral past, he sought and gained the Republican Party's nomination for the Ohio State Legislature in 1883. What happened at Sand Creek proved to be impossible for Chivington to overcome. His opponent made his inhumane behavior more than nineteen years earlier a major issue in the election.[27]

The political tactics were particularly effective in Clinton County, Ohio, where Chivington was a resident. A large number of Quakers lived in the area. Not only did they object to war in all forms but they also considered themselves the special guardians of the Indians. Voters voiced their opinions about the scandal-ridden parson-turned-business-owner in newspapers throughout Ohio. According to the August 24, 1883, edition of the *Lebanon Patriot*, Chivington was accused of campaigning with "the Gospel in one hand and a flaming Indian sword in the other."[28]

An unsigned letter in the August 17, 1883, edition of the *Clinton County Democrat* was equally condemning:

> Chivington is patronizing, oily-tongued, and understands to perfection the art of dissembling. Hypocrisy and deceit are distinguished characteristics of his being. Virtue and honor are strangers to his moral character. Under the cloak of religion he seeks to hide the deformity of his moral nature. While professing better things, and falsely claiming to be a laborer in the Master's vineyard, he has dishonored religion by committing deeds which, when brought under the searching influence of the moral horoscope, stand out, so conspicuously as dark and damning

blotches, that make him unfit to represent a people celebrated for integrity, prosperity, and honor.[29]

Figure 9.2. Plains Indian prisoners gather in front of the chapel for a photograph at the northeast corner of the prison, circa 1867. State Archives of Florida, *Florida Memory*

Figure 9.3.   Richard Henry Pratt was the founder of the Carlisle Indian Industrial School at Carlisle, PA. He
endent of education at Fort Marion prison during Mochi's stay there. Library of Congress LC-USZ62-26798

Chivington was asked by the nominating committee to withdraw from the race. He reluctantly did so but cited as the reason an unscrupulous opponent who was spreading rumors about him. An article in the October 8, 1883, edition of the *Daily Denver Times* quotes Chivington as saying, "One end of our country is settled very largely by Quakers, and when this story was brought out against me, it hurt me with them, for it seems as if they would prefer to vote for the incarnate fiend rather than for a man who had in any way hurt their peculiar pets, the Indians."[30]

Although Chivington had decided never again to run for public office, he continued to accept requests for public speaking. One such invitation came in mid-September 1883. The occasion was the twenty-fifth anniversary of the settlement of Colorado. Many distinguished leaders who played a part in settling the region were on hand to welcome the controversial man.[31]

When Chivington arrived at the reception, he was greeted with a round of applause and enthusiastic cheers. In addition to the supporters were a number of people who thought of Chivington as a "butcher." He made no apologies to the critics in the audience. "But were not these Indians peaceable?" He sarcastically asked the captivated crowd somewhere in the middle of his speech. "Oh, yes, peaceable! Well a few hundred of them have been peaceable for almost nineteen years, and none of them has been so troublesome as they were before Sand Creek." He continued:

> What are the facts? How about the treaty that Governor John Evans did not make with them in the summer of 1864. He, with the usual corps of attaches, under escort, went out to meet the Kiowa. When he got there they had done a day's march further out on the plains and would meet him there, and so on day after day they moved out as he approached, until wearied and suspicious of treachery, he returned without succeeding in his mission of peace.[32]
>
> He told them by message that he had a present for them, but it was not peace they wanted but war and plunder. What of the trains captured? Of supplies and wagons burned and carried off and killed? Aye, what of the scalps of white men, women, and children, several of which they had not time to dry and tan since taking. These, all these and more were taken from the belts of the dead warriors on the battlefield of Sand Creek, and from their tepees which fell into our hands.[33]
>
> What of the Indian blanket that was captured fringed with white women's scalps? What say the sleeping dust of the . . . men, women,

children, ranchers, emigrants, herders, and soldiers who lost their lives at the hands of these Indians? Peaceable? Now we are peaceably disposed, but decline giving such testimonials of our peaceful proclivities, and I say here, as I said in my home town in the Quaker County of Clinton, Ohio, in a speech one night last week, "I stand by Sand Creek."

According to information passed down through generations of Cheyenne Indians, Mochi spent most of her days at Fort Marion staring out at the vast ocean beyond the barred prison windows thinking of her days at Sand Creek. She never ceased to mourn the loss of her family or her former way of life, and she would not forsake her heritage regardless of the punishment she received for speaking the Cheyenne language and observing her own religion. Mochi could not be persuaded to put out of her mind the way the Cheyenne tribe she belonged to was killed. She longed to be with her loved ones and prepared herself for the death she thought was inevitable as an Indian captive. [34]

10

NEVER TO BE HOME AGAIN

Residents and tourists in the southern Florida town of St. Augustine gathered at the Magnolia Hotel on March 4, 1878, for an evening of entertaining presentations by the Indian prisoners from Fort Marion. Cheyenne inmates demonstrated a traditional dance performed at the summer solstice. Some of the Indians wore headdresses made with feathers to represent an eagle, and others wore hides over their shoulders to represent the buffalo. The eagle symbolized the spirit, and the buffalo symbolized the body. The dance served as a reminder of how important the buffalo was to the Plains Indians. [1]

The enthusiastic audience applauded the exhibition and many of the Cheyenne Indians watching the performance followed suit. Mochi was one of a handful of people that did not clap; remembering how few buffalo were left and how the Indians' lives had changed as a result made them fiercely unhappy. At the conclusion of the program, the audience filtered out of the main auditorium into the lobby to look over the various items on display made by the Fort Marion prisoners. Shells, drawings, bows, and arrows were available for purchase. [2]

Many Indians made money from curio sales. Some used the funds to buy postcards and watermelons. Many Cheyenne Indians turned their earnings over to prison officials and entrusted them to send the funds to their families living on reservations. More often than not, corrupt guards would steal the meager funds. [3]

Figure 10.1.   Mochi poses for a picture alongside her husband, Medicine Water, and three unidentified Chey
ring their incarceration at Fort Marion. Mochi is standing at the top left; Medicine Water is standing next
as taken circa 1877. Courtesy of Castillo de San Marcos & Fort Matanzas, St. Augustine, Florida, National P

Mochi and several other rebellious Indians, including Medicine Water, refused to participate in the souvenir-selling enterprise. They resented being imprisoned and were concerned only with the day they would be released. Some Cheyenne had difficulty believing they would ever be free and plotted their individual releases. Indians tried to escape on makeshift rafts or by lowering themselves down the high prison walls to the open sea. Many died in their attempts to be free. Warriors like Mochi were convinced such deaths were honorable compared to living a lifetime in captivity.[4]

In the fall of 1876, a severe type of typho-malarial fever claimed the lives of seventeen Indians at Fort Marion. In October an influential Cheyenne leader at the prison named Heap of Birds died of congestion and heart disease. Those closest to the one-time chief noted his greatest desire was to rejoin his family on the plains. His desire was shared by all the Indians interned at the stone stockade. An attitude of melancholy and hopelessness filled the hearts of the Native American captives. The administrators in charge of the prison were aware of the despair that had overtaken many of the Indians, and urged the government to intercede before all perished.[5]

According to a report issued by Ezra A. Hayt, commissioner of Indian affairs, to William T. Sherman, secretary of war, on November 10, 1877, Hayt suggested that serious changes be made to keep the Indians alive. "Their suffering seems to have been of sufficient severity for all reformatory purposes," Hayt wrote. "Severe punishment may have been, and probably was, visited upon some who were innocent of deliberate crimes, and a part of them have died away from their family and friends and of those remaining many are sick." Although Hayt acknowledged their good behavior, he expressed no remorse for their agony. "Believing that no possible interest would be served by their further imprisonment," he concluded, "I respectfully recommend that all these prisoners be returned to their tribes and released."[6]

In April 1878, the United States government approved Commissioner Hayt's suggestion to send the Indians to the Darlington Indian Agency. On April 17, the long journey from Florida to Oklahoma began. Colonel Nelson Miles, the same military officer who oversaw the Indians' transfer to Fort Marion, was placed in charge of escorting the Indians to the reservation. Thirty-seven-year-old Mochi was ill when she made the twenty-three-day trip to the setting the Cheyenne and Arapaho Indians were to call home. She had contracted tuberculosis while in prison and was struggling with a fever and coughing blood.[7]

The April 19, 1878, edition of the *Indianapolis Journal* contained an article about the transfer of the prisoners and noted that with the "exception of a certain few the worst desperados were being returned civilized and intelligent." According to the article, when the Indians passed through Indianapolis they attracted a great deal of attention. Citizens turned out by the hundreds to get a look at the many braves and the warrior woman. "These same prisoners who were sent to Florida chained and pinioned are now being released but their bloodthirsty nature has been reformed," the report read. Army officer R. H. Pratt was credited with transforming the Indians, including one female known as the "ruthless slayer of the German family." The article continued:

> Captain Pratt is a native of Indiana, and is now enjoying a respite from his official duties and visiting with his sister in this fair city. In conversation with a journal reporter last evening, Captain Pratt stated many interesting circumstances and reported the entire success of the experiment which had been tried on this company of Indian desperados. The captain used all kindly means to induce them to change their modes of life. He gradually succeeded in persuading them to abandon the use of a blanket as an article of clothing and wear half military dress which had been provided for them by the government. Then classes were organized for giving those who deemed to learn a rudimentary education, and most of them availed themselves of the opportunity offered. The older men made but little progress, but those under thirty years of age made, in some cases, excellent progress. And now, three years since education was introduced to the Indian, they are prepared for civilized life. Some men stayed on in Florida to continue learning; the older men have for the most part returned to their tribes, but it is believed their characteristics have been entirely changed.
>
> Captain Pratt does not make any comment expressive of his views on the Indian question but simply gives the facts as related above and leaves them to make their own impress. His testimony as to the remarkable change wrought in these apparently desperate and hardened Indians.[8]

With or without an education, former Fort Marion prisoners found it hard to readjust to life outside of jail. Their difficulty was not only becoming reacquainted with being free, but also adjusting to freedom on the government's terms. Indians were confined to the Oklahoma reservations, and they were not allowed to organize hunting parties. They had no money and no livestock, a situation that was particularly difficult to accept for the Cheyenne because they measured wealth in terms of horses. The government wanted the Indians to be farmers and teachers, to bring up a younger generation to read and write English, and to focus solely on the white man's vision for the Indians. They were to depend entirely on rations government agents issued. The system was fraught with corruption, and, as a result, Cheyenne leaders complained that the tribes were "often hungry and always poor."[9]

According to the October 20, 1878, edition of the *Indianapolis Journal*, Cheyenne Indians were leaving the reservation to find food. Cavalry leaders informed officials in Washington that there were too few troops to keep the Indians contained. General John Pope, commander of the Department of Missouri, was one of the first officers to learn that the daily Cheyenne Indian trouble was because the provisions promised were not being given to them. The *Indianapolis Journal* reported on the tumultuous situation:

> There is an enormous deficiency in Indian supplies. The daily rations of one and a half pounds of beef, a half-pound of flour or corn, and four pounds of coffee, eight pounds of sugar, and three pounds of beans in each hundred rations had only been partially carried out. None of the stock and aid in building their houses, which was promised, has been afforded them.
>
> Another cause of the problems with the Indians was that they objected to the manner of serving their rations. General Pope suggests that the Indian commissioner may, in the light of these facts, find it necessary to modify his view of affairs at the agency and instead of sending more troops to keep the Cheyenne on the reservation launch an investigation into the corruption that has taken place.[10]

Lack of health care was yet another issue that plagued the Indians. Those like Mochi who suffered from life-threatening illnesses received little to no medical attention and were not allowed to leave the reservation for help. "The Indian has no right[s] which the white man are bound to respect," an article in the April 15, 1880, issue of the Dearborn, Indiana, newspaper the *Dearborn County Register* noted regarding medical treatment for Native Americans. "If he submits to the white man's authority he is starved by hunger, disease, and cold united; if he is too proud to submit, and rebels, the military is employed to massacre him and his family."[11]

In late 1881, Mochi died from tuberculosis. She was forty-one years old. The traditional service for a Cheyenne Indian warrior who had passed began when his body was laid on a scaffold in tall trees. The belief was that resting on a high scaffold aided in the journey across the four great rivers. The four great rivers were bodies of water that combined to transport the deceased to the place of the dead called Seyon. Water from Sand Creek is said to have flowed into the great rivers. Weapons, jewelry, and a variety of gifts were left at the burial site so the deceased could use them in the afterlife. There were no trees in the area of Oklahoma where Mochi died, so she was buried on a high mound in order to find her way to Seyon. In Seyon she would be reunited with the friends and family that were slain at the Sand Creek Massacre, and they would live in the camp of the dead forever.[12]

Medicine Water was devastated by his wife's passing but found a way to work through his sorrows with a job as a reservation police officer. His position and those of the other Indian law enforcement agents ended in 1883 due to lack of funds.[13]

In 1926, more than forty years after losing Mochi, Medicine Water passed away. The late John L. Sipes, tribal historian for the Cheyenne Nation, noted in the April 2008 edition of *Wild West Magazine* that "death and the will to fight ran strong in the lives of Mochi and Medicine Water." He added that "the Old Ones [ancestors] have taught us that to endure the hardships of surviving, while maintaining love and courage to stand beside each other in overwhelming odds, was tremendous. In the end, it was the love and dedication to their people, their family, and their Cheyenne way of life that saw them through."[14]

Medicine Water was ninety years old when he died.

11

THE SAND CREEK MASSACRE HISTORIC SITE

Tribal leaders today in and around Chivington, Colorado, maintain they hear the cries of the children that were slaughtered on the banks of the Sand Creek in the winter of 1864. It was there that a unit led by Col. John M. Chivington led an unprovoked, early morning raid on an American Indian village, killing more than 150 Cheyenne and Arapahos, mostly women, children, and elderly men.

For more than a century no signs marked the location of the U.S. Calvary massacre that took place on November 29, 1864, but legislation passed in November 2000 made the area 160 miles southeast of Denver a national historic site.

Efforts to make the location a national site began in late 1990 when a project team was organized to study the area. On the banks of Sand Creek in Kiowa County, Colorado, an archeological team that included tribal members, National Park Service staff, historians, volunteers, and local landowners found evidence of the Indian village that was attacked by the U.S. Army. The team swept the area with metal detectors and found evidence of the horrific struggle. Among the shattered plates, utensils, hide scrapers, awls, and trade items that were once part of the daily lives of almost five hundred Indian people, the survey team also found fragments of the weapons used to attack and kill them.

According to the report prepared by the National Park Service in cooperation with the Cheyenne and Arapaho Tribes of Oklahoma, the Northern Cheyenne Tribe, the Northern Arapaho Tribe, and the state of

Colorado, a multi-disciplinary approach was used in finding the massacre site:

> As part of the site location effort, Cheyenne and Arapaho descendants of the Sand Creek Massacre told stories that had been handed down to them through the generations, including traditional tribal knowledge about the location of the site. Historians researched maps, diaries, reminiscences, and congressional and military investigative reports for information that might shed light on where the Sand Creek Massacre occurred. The National Park Service also held public open houses, encouraging local residents to come forward with information, including possible evidence of the massacre that had been found on their land. Historic aerial photographs, the earliest dating to the 1930s, were examined for evidence of historic trails that led to and from the massacre site. The site location effort also included a geomorphological assessment of Sand Creek that identified, through an analysis of soil samples, those specific landforms where 1864-era artifacts could potentially be recovered.
>
> Although most accounts of the Sand Creek Massacre placed it at the "Big South Bend" of Sand Creek, its exact location was obscured through time. Following the massacre, the Indian survivors could not even return to the site—which bordered on the Cheyenne and Arapaho reservation—to bury their dead. Located in what is still one of the most rural areas of Colorado, the massacre site was left untended. By the turn of the century, there was little evidence of the terrible event. In 1908, Army veterans who participated in the massacre planned a reunion at the site. However, upon reaching the banks of the Sand Creek, even they could not agree as to its location.

On Saturday, April 28, 2007, after more than eight years of research and study, a thousand people, including victims' descendants, gathered on the rolling plains in Kiowa County for the official dedication of the Sand Creek Massacre National Historic Site. A mock village of seventeen teepees was set up in a stand of cottonwood trees along the creek, where historians believe the slaughter took place. According to the April 29, 2007, news story by the *Associated Press*, "Cheyenne and Arapaho tribes who attended the ceremony chanted and played drums. Tribal members who were Army veterans wore their camouflage uniforms as well as headdresses when they carried in the U.S. and tribal flags."

Although it took more than a century to build a memorial, the attack was recognized almost immediately as criminal. Congress condemned it, and President Lincoln fired territorial Governor John Evans.

Witnesses told a congressional hearing that the victims had not been hostile. Indian trader John S. Smith testified that Chivington knew the band at Sand Creek was peaceful and was not involved in the attacks on settlers.

But after the raid Chivington was feted as a hero by Denver residents who were terrified that the Confederacy would use the Indians as surrogates to wage war on them.

A Civil War memorial installed at the Colorado capital in 1909 listed Sand Creek as a great Union victory. But a plaque was added in 2002 giving details of the massacre to set the record straight.

The inclusion of the site within the national park system provides an important reminder of a key event in western American history.

For more information about the Sand Creek Massacre National Site visit www.nps.gov.

EPILOGUE

Colonel John Chivington died of stomach cancer on October 4, 1894, at the age of seventy. His life after his speech at the twenty-fifth anniversary of the settlement of Colorado until he passed away was busy. Chivington moved to Denver in 1893, continuing to write for the Methodist newspaper *The Christian Advocate*. He also served as a coroner and deputy sheriff. [1]

Chivington was involved in several lawsuits over land given to him by the United States government that was located in El Paso County, Colorado. The land encompassed the boiling soda springs later known as Manitou Springs. During Chivington's sixteen-year absence from the territory his land had been sold to entrepreneurs who wanted to bottle the water from the springs. Chivington had given his son-in-law, Thomas Pollack, power of attorney of the property in February 1867. His son-in-law sold the coveted land six months later for $500. [2]

Although Chivington mounted an aggressive fight to recover the property he claimed ultimately belonged to him, the Supreme Court of Colorado struck down his case. The court argued that he had not paid taxes on the land or exercised any rights of ownership for sixteen years and, as such, "the legal property owners were the individuals who did maintain fiscal responsibility." [3]

On July 21, 1891, Chivington applied for a "disabled pension" from the government. He claimed that injuries he had suffered while serving in the army in 1864 had left him unable to make a living. Chivington died before his application was approved. [4]

Colonel Chivington's well-attended funeral was held on October 7, 1894, at the Trinity Methodist-Episcopal Church. News of his demise and the funeral service was published in newspapers as far away as London. "He was a noted character in Colorado history," an article in the November 9, 1894, edition of the *American Register* reported. "He was born in Ohio in 1821 and went to Missouri in early life as a minister of the Methodist Church. As such he went to Colorado in 1862, also entering the Volunteers, in which he was made colonel. In the winter of 1863 he led the Colorado troops in the famous Sand Creek Massacre. The people of Colorado congratulated Colonel Chivington for his work, but the government did not approve of what it termed an 'Indian massacre.'"[5]

The controversial parson was laid to rest at the Fairmount Cemetery in Denver.

The four young girls who survived being captured by Cheyenne Indians in the fall of 1874 left Fort Sill, Oklahoma, in the summer of 1875 to live in Leavenworth, Kansas. Congress made provisions for the care of Catherine, Sophia, Julia, and Adelaide by appropriating $2,500 for each one of them. According to Catherine German's memoirs, the interest derived from the sum of money was to be used for "maintenance and education." The money for the orphans was taken from the United States government appropriations for the Cheyenne Indians.[6]

The girls were cared for by two guardians, one of whom was General Nelson Miles. He made sure all four attended school and graduated. On October 1, 1875, an article in the *Lawrence Republican Daily* let concerned citizens know how the girls were doing. "The German sisters are very happy in their new home with Mrs. Wilson near Lawrence," the report read. "It is a quiet, pleasant place to live. They attend school near at hand, and are enjoying peace and comfort after their terrible suffering among the wild Cheyenne."[7]

After high school Julia attended the Teacher's Institute and received a certificate to teach. Adelaide continued her education at State University in Lawrence, Kansas. All the German sisters married and each had children. Adelaide settled in Missouri, Sophia in Nebraska, and Julia and Catherine made California their home. They were all in their early seventies when they passed away, and all of them died from natural causes. Adelaide was the last sister to die. The March 7, 1943, edition of the *Pampa News* reported that she passed away at her home in Kansas City,

Missouri, in January 1943 at the age of seventy-four. The article included information about a journey the four sisters took together in 1928 to the location where they were rescued in 1875.[8]

General Nelson Miles was the guardian of the German sisters for more than a year. He resigned his position when the military ordered him into the Northwest Country to end the war between the hostile Sioux, Nez Perce, and Bannock Indians, and the United States. The celebrated army chief died on May 15, 1925, in Washington, D.C., while attending a circus performance. "When I learned of his death," Catherine German wrote in her memoirs, "I grieved as though he were a near and dear relative."[9]

According to the May 16, 1925, edition of the *Daily News*, "Miles was a brave commander who passed through numerous engagements during the Civil War unscathed." Although only twenty-four years old when the Civil War ended, Miles had become famous in army circles, and Generals Grant, Meade, Hooker, and Hancock, and every other field officer under whom he served, urged he be promoted. He was honored with the Congressional Medal.[10]

General Miles's Indian service began in 1870. He then embarked on campaigns that were to bring to a close the Indian Wars which lasted throughout the country. In 1894, Miles was called to subdue the historic Chicago railroad strike. President Cleveland rewarded the general's distinguished services by appointing him commanding general of the United States Army.

General Miles was eighty-six when he died.

Civil War veteran R. H. Pratt was in charge of the education of Indian prisoners at Fort Marion from 1875 to 1878. He and a small staff of teachers taught the inmates how to read and write English. In 1879 Pratt moved to Pennsylvania, where he founded the Carlisle Indian Industrial School. By combining academics with vocational training in a variety of fields, Pratt was able to place students in non-Native American homes and colleges. The school grew steadily, and in his twenty-five years as superintendent he had charge of more than five thousand children of more than seventy tribes.[11]

Often called "the Red Man's Moses," Pratt is attributed with leading the Indian out of the desert of reservation bondage into the promised land of citizenship and opportunity. He died while visiting friends in San Francisco on March 15, 1924. He was laid to rest in Arlington National Cemetery along with his wife, Anna.[12]

The Fort Marion prison was officially closed in 1900. Notorious Apache Indian leader Geronimo was one of the last to be held there. In October 1966 the prison was added to the National Register of Historic Places and renamed Castillo de San Marco.[13]

The spot where more than 150 Southern Cheyenne and Arapaho were slaughtered along Big Sandy, southeast of Denver, Colorado, became a national historic site in September 2001. A plaque at the location reminds visitors of the event that happened there in November 1864. The Sand Creek Massacre remains one of the most tragic incidents of the Indian Wars.[14]

REMEMBERING SAND CREEK

The history of the men and women that blazed the trails to and settled the untamed West was documented by hundreds of thousands of individuals who experienced the adventure. Homesteaders and their families, trappers and explorers, soldiers and their wives, school teachers and their students were just a few who recorded their journeys. Written accounts of notable events, from the discovery of gold in California and Colorado to the building of the transcontinental railroad, have been preserved in libraries and universities. Archive departments in cities and towns across the United States contain mountains of records of the comings and goings of those who made their way into a wild wilderness and did whatever they could to tame it.

Unlike the early Americans who chronicled everything that occurred, the Indians shared accounts of their history orally. Some of the Indians' history has been written down, but in large part the experience of being an Indian is based in recollection; it is in the stories retained and traditions remembered and passed along from generation to generation. Indian tribes across the United States depend on their oral history to sustain their culture. Sharing the experiences of the leaders and members of the Indian tribes who came before, and describing their triumphs and struggles, preserves the rich heritage of the Indian Nations.

In the early 1990s, Alan McEachern, chief justice of the British Columbia Supreme Court, ruled on many cases involving various claims Indian tribes had on land from Toronto to Quebec and noted in judgment briefs the issue he had with the Indian's oral history. The March 12, 1991, edition of the Medicine Hat News reported that the chief justice wrote: "Indians have a romantic view of their history . . . it's without literal or legal value."[1] *Among those who have sought to change that perception are Cheyenne Indian historian John Stands in Timber and anthropologist Margo Liberty.*[2] *The pair collaborated on books that record the legendary times of the Cheyenne. Their work and that of American history professors, students from the National American Indian Data Center, and countless others in the field of Indian studies show that the Indians' oral history has great merit.*

Research projects, like the one launched by the National Park Service and tribal representatives for the Cheyenne and Arapaho Indians in the year 2000 about the Sand Creek Massacre, demonstrate that the Indians' oral history is anything but romantic. Recollections of the survivors of the massacre that occurred in the winter of 1864 have been shared with members of the tribes for over a century.[3] *The following are a few of those tattered and tragic memories.*

* * *

When the people were running there was hardly any place to hide, but there were ravines and there was one old lady who was getting children. She was getting children but she had medicine so they couldn't see her and she would go back and forth getting children. There were more women holding the children down. Where it happened had to have shelter and some ravines. Land changes over the years through men tilling, farmers, and the wind, rain—it changes subtly. Those ravines might be buried now. To find anything you'd probably have to dig. But at the time there were hiding places, ravines. They were camped close to water for cooking and things.

Lettie June Shakespeare

That old man, when he had his camp—Chief White Antelope—he had his camp and then this cavalry, they came and they seen those horses and flags. They didn't think much. My grandpa he took that white flag and when they got close to him they killed them all even though they had the flag. One woman got away with her grandson. She was the only one that lived through the massacre.

Josephine White

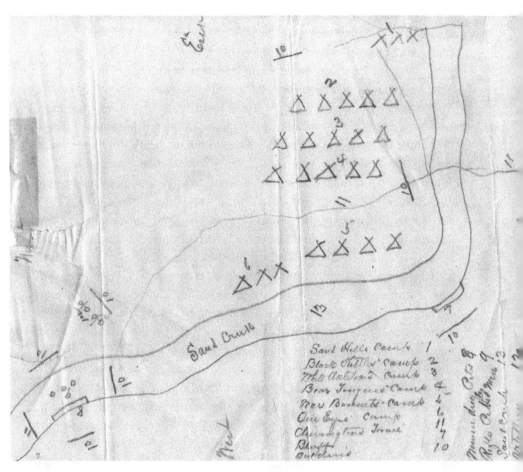

11.1.   Original map drawn by Cheyenne warrior George Bent, which shows the location of the Indian's te
el Chivington and the United States Volunteers attacked the tribes at the Sand Creek Massacre. Research
klahoma Historical Society

Some old men, some chiefs, wanted to make peace with the U.S. government. They had a meeting, they really trusted white men. Once they
become a chief, they must be honest and sincere and love their people and
help them in good ways. Once they become chief they can't argue with
anyone. If someone hurts them they've got to take their pipe and smoke.
That's all they could do. So, these two old men, Black Kettle and another
one . . . Sitting Bear . . . they went a few days before to soldier camp to
make peace and when they came back to the village somebody told them
the soldier would come back to attack them. And they said, "No they
won't, we were there to make peace with the soldiers (blue coats)." They
didn't take their words of warning, once you make peace with somebody
they take it seriously. "You should move," [the chiefs were told. The
chiefs said,] "No, they won't hurt us." But the next day they came, the
blue coats, shooting at them. When they started shooting, Black Kettle
and White Antelope got the flag, I guess they had gotten it from the
soldiers. Somebody told them to wave it so the soldiers wouldn't attack.
So they did, they raised the flag. But the blue coats destroyed it and then
started shooting at them. They scattered out, the women and children, and
tried to hide in the banks. One woman was pregnant and started to run
and jumped into the bank and the baby was born. Another woman jumped
in and got that baby to take care of it. My husband's relatives—his grandma's son—came running and jumped into the bank. His religion was
Clowns, or Backwards, it was religion, not in a funny way. He came and
jumped in and the woman, the nurse said, "No, you've come to the wrong
place." He saw that a baby was born and he jumped out because he's
backwards, that means he was happy seeing the baby. He started to run
off but the soldiers shot him down. Next was my husband's grandma . . .
she got shot down at the tepee and they cut her up everywhere. She was
still breathing and alive.

Blanche White Shield

What they describe as the ravines . . . when the first attack came everyone
scattered, the old ones and the women. Throughout the first day and
maybe even the second day, there were riders who were going to the
trouble of hunting down the wounded and finishing them off. I even heard
that the next day they were tracking them down. There was obviously a
lot going on in every direction, I don't know how many soldiers there

were but they were spending a lot of time in the creek bed area. Others, like outriders, were to the different directions. When I see what's there it seems that you'd only need horseback to the south and west, because it seems like other directions are within sight. There's nowhere to hide, it's flat to the east of the site with terrain to the south and the west of the site. To the north, I guess that's where there's a question about the pits. I know you all have thought about it but if you've ever been under gunfire, you're not gonna want to run two or three miles. I can tell you for a fact you're not going to run very far under gunfire. Unless you have complete disregard for your own safety, then you might run a quarter of a mile or a few hundred yards, but with that many guns, you're not going to run very far. I can't imagine they're going to run two or three miles. If you've been under gunfire you know what I'm talking about. Maybe one lucky person could get even a quarter of a mile, because they're going to get you one way or another. The pits had to be nearby. Besides, you can't dig into that hard terrain, not with the kind of tools they would have had. Back in those days they had big caliber guns. I've heard about these pits, I would call them foxholes, but they'd have to be within a very short distance of the site. I heard they were on the run from the initial attack, they scattered and the army did a mop-up. Those that scattered—a lot of wounded and elderly looking for their children and the next day the soldiers were riding up and down the ravines picking them off. I'm sure under the cover of darkness some of them got away too.

Arleigh Rhodes

The soldiers mutilated the dead. Some of them didn't die immediately. They were wounded and the soldiers stayed there and finished killing them the next day. I've heard different stories from different families. One was from a family about a little girl whose mother got a horse and was able to grab the little girl by the arm and pull her up and they got away. And then this lady, Mrs. Starr, told me that her great-great-grand-mother was a little girl and she was covered up in a hole, covered with sand and leaves, and she survived. Then Laird had a story about two small children whose father managed to catch a horse and put his two small children on the horse and got them out of there and told them to keep going. The kids kept switching the horse and they ran and ran till the horse died of exhaustion.

Colleen Cometsevah

My grandpa told the story about Standing Elk getting killed at Sand Creek. A government soldier was shooting at him and that's how he got killed. He fought back with bows and arrows. He wasn't married then. My grandpa Morning Star also got away from Sand Creek. He also went to Lame Deer. So many people on that side have stories about Sand Creek. So many Chiefs got away from Sand Creek, at least three. But they're not my kinfolk, they're on the other side. Morning Star was one of my great grandpas. Black Kettle got away too, but he got killed at Washita by Custer.

Jesse Howling Water

Everything at Sand Creek—horses, tepees, wagons—everything was destroyed. Set on fire. My relatives there were Greasy Nose and Black Bear. Their descendants are the White Turtles. There is only three White Turtles left. Even little babies, they shot them dead. This one old man he was standing on a hill, it was solid rock, straight down. He was calling to the people [in Cheyenne], saying "this way, this way" as people ran. There was an old lady, she had a baby and she was running (or riding?) to a man. But somebody shot her in the back of the head and she dropped the baby. But a man came by and scooped the baby up. Don't know what became of that baby.

Roger White Turtle

Their grandmother was a little girl at the time and her mother tried to run with her but she couldn't keep up. So she tried to carry her but the mother gave out as they were running up Sand Creek she just scooped out the sand and put her little girl there and told her not to move and that she'd be back for her. She covered her with sand and brush and leaves and ran off. When she came back two days later the little girl was still alive. The little girl suffered through that cold, with no cover, no food or water. Another one told me that their grandmother was running ahead of her mother and the mother managed to get hold of one of the horses. The little girl turned around and saw her and the little girl held out her arm and her mother reached down and scooped her up and they both got away.

Colleen Cometsevah

My father's parents were present at Sand Creek. This Sand Creek, to begin with, was a creek with pools of water, but no running water at the time of the massacre. At that time there was an accumulation of light snow in places. In the early morning hours, you can just begin to see in the morning light. Some young men's duties were to watch the horses, on both sides of Sand Creek. These horses were scattered on both sides of the creek. They didn't group their horses all together, they grouped them according to clan groups. These two young men, Little Bear and King-fisher, were the first to see this long line of soldiers coming from the south, moving along Sand Creek like a snake. They first thought it was buffalo, then realized it was an army group of some kind. The soldiers divided into two groups, like a horseshoe, to head off the horse herds on either side of the creek. Then Chivington's soldiers were walking in the center, and they were headed towards Black Kettle's camp. The 44 Chey-enne Chiefs Society, orphans, widows, and the elderly were in this en-campment. This is the group they brought down from Smokey Hill to Fort Lyon. They were told to go back to Sand Creek. They were glad and led to believe they would be under military protection. They were told to raise the American flag—Black Kettle was to raise it with the white flag of truce beneath it to indicate that they were peaceful.

When they were at Fort Lyon, they were also told to surrender all their weapons including pistols, rifles, bows and arrows. They hunted anything they could: deer, antelope, and sometimes buffalo.

When the troops were attacking Black Kettle's camp consisting of children, women, elders, widows, and orphans and the 44 Chiefs Soci-eties, the women, children and elders ran toward the bluff on the west end of the encampment. Some were killed there. Others ran upstream, but didn't get far. Soldiers on horseback caught up with them and they had to dig pits for protections. These last pits were about one mile north of the southwest corner of South Bend of the Dawson's property.

By tribal law, the 44 Chiefs Societies must protect their people and give their lives so their people can escape. That is why so many of the chiefs were killed. My great-grandfather was a young chief at the time and he ran to where Black Kettle raised the flag. White Antelope and others were there also. The troops opened fire on them. They said the troops came like a horseshoe from the east part of the camp area where it turns back south downstream to the Arkansas River. They came from that direction like a horseshoe and went upstream. The chiefs stood their ground and the troops concentrated their gunfire on the lodges. Later, people said the bullets sounded like hail hitting the lodges. They fired directly into the lodges knowing that people would still be asleep, especially the elders and young children. As the chiefs held the soldiers off, the chiefs slowly moved back. I was told that these young men's duty was watching the horses. Kingfisher and Little Bear, who had gone after their horses early, these two ran back to the camp and warned everyone as best they could that the soldiers were coming. But when the troops got to the east end of where the bend goes back south to the Arkansas river, the camp was attacked horseshoe fashion. When George Bent saw this, he ran west to the high bluff by where the marker is now. He saw that a group of young men was standing there trying to decide what to do. At that point, George Bent mentioned it was about one hundred yards from the encampment. So it meant to me that they were camped all the way over by the bluff by where the marker is and back east. At this bluff the women and children dug what they call sandpits or rifle pits, but I call them survival pits. They dug in at the middle of the channel. From there the chiefs stood their ground. My great-grandfather said when the troops quit shooting at them the sun was straight up. Somewhere between the bluff and the first sandpit George Bent got shot in the hip, but he survived in the sandpit.

Cheyenne they all belong to family clans, clan groups where all their relatives camped together and each one of them has a name. They each belong to one of these four military societies: Bowstring, Elk, Kit Fox, [and] Dog Soldier . . . the Chief Society being the governing body of the Cheyenne. All the other societies are subordinate to the chiefs, the governing system of 44 Cheyenne chiefs. They are the ones that make all the decisions for the Cheyenne Tribe. Whatever is decided is enforced by the Bowstring Society. They can tear down your lodge, destroy your belongings and kill your horses and dogs, they enforce what the chiefs decide and dictate.

Laird Cometsevah

This story starts with the morning attack by the troops of Chivington. It happened real early in the morning and my grandfather had just gotten up, hadn't even started the fire. First thing he thought of was his rawhide rope. He was more concerned about his wife who was pregnant at that time with my oldest uncle. My grandfather ran out of the tepee and it

Figure 11.2. This photograph is of the only child saved out of the Sand Creek Massacre. The Denver Public Library, Western History Collection, Z-1513

happened that the horses were running by the tepee so he roped one of the horses, he stopped it, brought it to his tepee, and told my grandmother to get ready, she was going for a ride out of the battle. My grandmother got ready while he was fixing the horse, got her on a horse and [he] told her to go back the direction where the horse went and she did. She caught up to the horses and this is how she got through the lines in the midst of these horses going through the battle. And my grandfather went back into the tepee, grabbed his weapon, bows and arrows and maybe rifle that he had which he didn't tell me, but anyway he came out, starting to fight his way out of the battle. And one main thing he tells about, the incident that happened while he was fighting his way out, there was a blind man with a medicine pouch, carrying it in the back, and the old man was blind, and a little kid was guiding him to safety. And my grandfather stopped by to care for the old man and he got wounded while doing this, got hit in the elbow. But then he had to get away because he was bleeding, and left the old man. He didn't know if he was killed or what but he left the old man there and fought his way out of the battle with a wounded arm, and he got away.

Ray Brady

When that incident came, when the army attacked the village, [it] prob-ably ignored the flag and they tried to stop them and said we are peaceful Indians, we are the peaceful tribe. We do not wish to fight. But still, they insist to fight them. Whatever they had was to defend themselves, but it's not enough. The army was too heavily armed to try to defend themselves. They were slaughtered. A lot of kids were killed trying to run for cover. They could not make it to the edge of the bank where it's close by the camp; they all got caught. But somehow my grandmother's great-grand-mother was six years old. I cannot remember the name she had. She managed to run and made it to the creek bottom. As she hid on the side of the bank where a lot of this grass was hanging over the edge, sat there and according to her story, she listened till she heard the last cry of the last wounded person gasping for life until finally there was silence. There were still people there suffering in agony from the soldiers, from their bullets, from their swords. I don't know how long she was there, but she finally managed to leave in the dark. Because she wanted to go back and see who all was killed; but, according to her story, when she looked back, everything was destroyed. The tepees were burned. Kids all were laying scattered, butchered, scalped, so she ran and ran. I don't know how many days she ran, how she got to Red Cloud Agency.

Donlin Many Bad Horses

Our old folks told us about the massacre. It's sad that our people had to struggle to live. They were industrious, good workers, knew how to survive. They were buffalo hunters and moved after the buffalo and got their supply of food. Also berries and digging for vegetables. . . . When they had this massacre, they had to defend themselves. They had to hunt. The women tanned hides and took care of the children while the men were out getting food. If fences weren't up you could go anywhere and dig medicine.

The U.S. Army settled and had a camp there after the treaty. The government broke the treaty. If we could get the place in Colorado back, that was our home place, but they had that massacre because of the silver and gold—the minerals.

You know that Shoshone and Arapaho massacre [happened] because they broke the treaty. My grandfather was there. In one night they just killed . . . Chief Black Coal, he was there. He had one finger missing. He signed a treaty with Chief Washakie. They saw he was a Flathead, but he was married into Shoshone. Broken Hand had his hand shot in the massacre. My dad was shot in the massacre. He was shot in the heart and died. Elmer Iron. That was my maiden name. His Arapaho name meant iron, or steel, or money, I don't know.

They used to tie the horses on the alert. Didn't trust, you know. My mother's brother got shot and killed right there. He broke his back. They shot him. He jumped on his horse and my grandmother just ran and hid with her little ones. [They] just crawled in the bush.

Cleone Thunder

I said a prayer for the spirits that are still at Sand Creek because of the genocide that was forced upon them. The treaty they made with the Cheyenne and other tribes in 1851 included Denver, Wyoming, and other areas. But, when gold was discovered they needed to move the Indians out of the way, so in 1861 they moved the Cheyenne and Arapahos to the Sand Creek area. When the massacre occurred on November 29, 1864, the Cheyenne were on the reservation the U.S. government had given them, and the government condoned this action resulting in the killing of these innocent people.

Laird Cometsevah

Each evening my grandmother would start telling us the story about Sand Creek. I was just a little girl then and I didn't hardly catch all of it, but I'll tell what I can remember. She used to say that when they got attacked the men tried to protect them and told the women to take off, children and old men, and my grandfather was one of the protectors trying to protect them. And when my grandfather was still there waiting for all of them to get away my grandfather was using a bow and arrow trying to keep them soldiers back and he got wounded—I don't remember if it was the right or left arm—and afterwards they took off. He started taking off to follow the people, and there was a little boy walking around there that got left, he grabbed that little boy and took off with him. And when they were running they heard a whole bunch of horses coming, they thought the soldiers were catching up with them and here it was a stallion leading a whole bunch of horses. And it stopped for those people and those people went and grabbed whatever horses they wanted to get on. After they got on them horses that stallion took off again and led the horses and went like he went to hide them somewhere where they couldn't find them.

Nellie Bear Tusk

The soldiers gathered us from our camp along with the Cheyenne; the soldier chief told us that we were to be moved to our new [reservation] campground which was to become our new and permanent campground [new reservation].

We had a big herd of horses along with the Cheyenne and it took us several days to make the move. When we came to the new campground, the soldier chief told us to put up a white flag with their [American] flag so that any other soldiers would know that we were a friendly tribe and that they would not attack us and would leave us alone.

On the morning of the massacre I was awakened with the camp crier telling us to wake up; his words were "Wake up, Arapaho, the soldiers are attacking, the soldiers are attacking us! Run, scatter, run, scatter, we will all meet again in two moons where we had our last Sun Dance. We will all meet again where we had our last Sun Dance."

Being a young woman [girl], I sat up from my bed and put on my moccasins. There was an awful lot of noise outside the teepee. As I went outside the teepee I saw people running in every direction and I saw people falling down and teepees falling apart. The people falling down were those that were getting killed, the teepees falling apart were those getting hit from the soldier's big guns.

I started running toward the hills which were north of the camp. As I was running near some rocks I heard my name being called: "Singing Water, Singing Water." I stopped running and looked around and could not see anyone, I was about to start running again when this voice called my name again, "Singing Water, look up to the rocks, we are behind them. Crawl up here and we will hide you with us." I crawled up to the rocks where this voice came from, when I got to the rocks the man made an entrance for me. I had to stand up and climb over the rocks; behind the rocks were a man, woman, and a child. We stayed hidden behind the rocks for two days.

On the second night the man said "it's time for us to move" so we started north along the creek and walked all night. When it started to dawn the man said that we have to move away from the creek and hide all day till nightfall and continue our journey north. He said that they would walk and hide during the night. We walked for several nights and when the man thought it was safe enough, we started walking during the day. How we survived was that we dug up the roots that we knew were edible and also any berries that hadn't fallen off the bushes. Also we would sit above the prairie dog holes and knock them in the head and roast them.

By then we weren't afraid to make fires as it was getting cold. I don't remember how many days it took us to reach our gathering place. I do remember that the snow was already deep. The Arapahos that were there told of some of the people that were caught and some of the ones that were killed. We stayed at the gathering place for several more days then we moved further north. We stayed near the mountains to get any game animals for food and if the soldiers found us we could get away in the mountains.

Story of the Sand Creek Massacre as told to Warren children by their grandmother, Singing Under Water Moss.

I'll tell you what my grandmother told me a long time ago. When the army came in and started killing them. She said it was bad, they murdered them, tortured them, and the horses they were on, they were just dragging them, and everything was burned down. And her and her mother and her grandmother were running up the hill. And my grandfather's mom, that was Matt Sitting Eagle. And she said her mother was packing him, he was just a baby, about three or four years old. She got shot in that battle, in the shoulder, and he got nicked in his shoulder too. They got away and they had to wait till everything calmed down and they went back down there and there was a lot of wounded and some were dead and they buried them. And they had to leave from there because they couldn't sleep there . . . it was bad.

Evangeline C'Hair

They never really forgot what happened. They would cry whenever they told about Sand Creek. . . . When everyone started running the young ones would get lost. Those that hid watched the soldiers from their hiding place. During that time when it was almost over, soldiers came out and cut open the bellies of women who were going to have a child. When they cut the child out they cut his throat.

Emma Red Hat and William Red Hat, Jr.

The battle scattered people. . . . At Sand Creek, you can go there at any time of day or night and if you close your mind to everything else you can feel the children, where they're congregating and laughing and having fun. The old ladies mostly congregate in the shade. The young warriors congregate in the rocks.

Robert Toahty

I remember the story. It's about a little old lady. It was either her grand-son or probably an orphan boy. They lived together and she was camped on the outskirts of the main camp. So during the battle they weren't right in the midst of it. Her grandson grabbed a very stubborn horse or mule or maybe a donkey. I'm sure it was frightened too, but he tried to put his grandmother on the horse and she would fall off on the other side. I can imagine the frenzy, everything going on, bullets flying, screaming, and he was desperately trying to get his grandmother away. And she had a medi-cine bundle, I don't know if it was hers or someone else's, she had it on her back and he managed to get her on there and they got away from the battle. And as they were running or leaving and the bullets were flying around and she put her head forward and at that instant a bullet grazed her head and followed the top of her head.

Marie Sanchez

NOTES

INTRODUCTION

1. *Rocky Mountain News*, December 17, 1864.
2. *Harpers Weekly* 36, no. 18 (1868).
3. Ibid.
4. *Rocky Mountain News*, December 17, 1864.
5. Ibid.
6. *Kansas City Star*, October 16, 1927.
7. Ibid.

I. TRAGEDY AT LITTLE BLUE RIVER

1. Arrell Morgan Gibson, "St. Augustine Prisoners," *Red River Valley Historical Review* 3, 259–70; Brad D. Lookingbill, *War Dance at Fort Marion: Plains Indian War Prisoners*, 41–55.
2. Joe F. Taylor, *The Indian Campaign on the Staked Plains*, 279–80.
3. *Danville Republican*, December 22, 1910.
4. Patrick M. Mendoza, Ann Strange-Owl-Raben, and Nico Strange-Owl, *Four Great Rivers to Cross: Cheyenne History, Culture and Traditions*, 75–76.
5. Ibid., 57; Patrick M. Mendoza, *Song of Sorrow: Massacre at Sand Creek*, 163–64.
6. *Danville Republican*, December 22, 1910.
7. Mendoza et al., *Four Great Rivers to Cross*, 57–62.
8. Ibid.; Linda Wommack and John L. Sipes, Jr., "Mo-chi: First Female Cheyenne Warrior," *Wild West Magazine*, April 2000, 22–23.

9. Mendoza et al., *Four Great Rivers to Cross*, 57–62.

10. Grace Jackson Penney, *Tales of the Cheyennes*, 26–27.

11. John G. Ellenbecker, *The Little Blue River Tragedy*, 17–19.

12. *Marysville Advocate-Democrat*, December 2, 1926.

13. Ibid.

14. *Beatrice Daily Sun*, January 22, 1927.

15. *Logansport Journal*, November 5, 1884.

16. *Marysville Advocate-Democrat*, December 2, 1926.

17. Virginia N. Leasure, "The Captivity of Laura L. Roper," 16–17.

18. Ellenbecker, *Little Blue River Tragedy*, 23–25.

19. *Daily Rocky Mountain News*, September 13, 1865.

20. Ellenbecker, *Little Blue River Tragedy*, 21–31.

21. *Indianapolis Indiana State Guard*, March 23, 1861.

22. Ibid.

23. *Racine Weekly Advocate*, April 3, 1861; *Burlington Daily Hawk Eye*, August 13, 1862.

24. George E. Hyde, *Life of George Bent: Written from His Letters*, 73–76; *Galveston Flakes Daily Bulletin*, December 1, 1868; *Oxford Benton Tribune*, December 12, 1865.

25. Peter Harrison, *Mochi: Cheyenne Woman Warrior*, 5–6.

26. Ellenbecker, *Little Blue River Tragedy*, 25–32.

27. *Beatrice Daily Sun*, March 20, 1907.

28. *Lawton Constitution-Morning News*, February 10, 1957; Reginald S. Craig, *The Fighting Parson: Biography of Colonel John M. Chivington*, 141–43.

29. Craig, *Fighting Parson*; *Watchmen & Wesleyan Advertiser*, October 4, 1865.

30. Craig, *Fighting Parson*, 143–46.

31. Ibid., 189–91.

32. Hyde, *Life of George Bent*, 151–57.

33. Craig, *Fighting Parson*, 189–91.

34. *North Hills News Record*, September 15, 1971.

35. *Davenport Democrat*, May 3, 1929; *Life of George Bent*, 131–35.

36. *Life of George Bent*, 131–35; *North Hill News Record*, September 15, 1972.

37. Lookingbill, *War Dance at Fort Marion*, 58–61.

2. THE REVEREND COLONEL

1. *Logansport Daily Star*, March 2, 1874; *Danville Republican*, December 22, 1910.

2. Brad D. Lookingbill, *War Dance at Fort Marion: Plains Indian War Prisoners*, 56–60.

3. Ibid.; *Danville Republican*, December 22, 1910.

4. Grace Jackson Penney, *Tales of the Cheyennes*, 15–19.

5. Ibid., 26–35; Patrick M. Mendoza, Ann Strange-Owl-Raben, and Nico Strange-Owl, *Four Great Rivers to Cross: Cheyenne History, Culture and Traditions*, 11–18.

6. Mendoza et al., *Four Great Rivers to Cross*, 57–62.

7. George Bird Grinnell, "Some Early Cheyenne Tales," *Journal of American Folklore* 20, 171–73.

8. Ibid.

9. Peter Harrison, *Mochi: Cheyenne Indian Warrior*, 4–7.

10. Reginald S. Craig, *The Fighting Parson: Biography of Colonel John M. Chivington*, 159–60.

11. *Daily Rocky Mountain News*, August 10, 1864.

12. Ibid.

13. Craig, *Fighting Parson*, 159–60.

14. Ibid., 22–25.

15. John Speer, "Report to Fred Martin of Interview with Mrs. John Chivington"; Lori Cox-Paul, "John M. Chivington: The Reverend Colonel," 128–30.

16. Patricia Kinney Kaufman, *My Mother's People to Colorado They Came*, 21–24; *History of the Reverends John M. and Isaac Chivington in their Relationship to the Early Methodist Episcopal Church in Kansas and Nebraska*.

17. Craig, *Fighting Parson*, 29–33.

18. Ibid., 34–36.

19. Ibid.

20. Ibid., 34–35; John R. Swanton, *Indian Tribes of North America Bulletin*, 235.

21. Kaufman, *My Mother's People*, 23; Craig, *Fighting Parson*, 35.

22. Craig, *Fighting Parson*, 40–41.

23. Ibid.

24. Ibid., 42–44; Kaufman, *My Mother's People*, 22–23.

25. Kaufman, *My Mother's People*, 23–24; Craig, *Fighting Parson*, 43.

26. Craig, *Fighting Parson*, 65; Isaac H. Beardsley, *Echoes from Peak and Plain: Tales of Life, War, Travel, and Colorado Methodism*, 242.

27. Craig, *Fighting Parson*, 142.

28. Ibid., 110–14; *Las Vegas Daily Optic*, July 15, 1958.

29. Kaufman, *My Mother's People*, 25–28.

30. Ibid.; Craig, *Fighting Parson*, 144–46.

31. Craig, *Fighting Parson*, 154–57.

32. Ibid.; Robert H. Lowie, *Indians of the Plains*, 106–10.

33. Craig, *Fighting Parson*, 163–64.

34. George E. Hyde, *Life of George Bent: Written from His Letters*, 131–34; *Report of the Secretary of War Sand Creek Massacre*, Senate Executive Doc. No. 26, 169.

35. *Report of the Secretary of War Sand Creek Massacre*, Senate Executive Doc. No. 26, 87–91; Craig, *Fighting Parson*, 171–73.

36. Robert Vine and John Mack Faragher, *The American West: A New Interpretive History*, 228.

37. Craig, *Fighting Parsons*, 175–76; Kaufman, *My Mother's People*, 32–33.

38. Penney, *Tales of the Cheyennes*, 45–52.

39. Ibid.

40. Ibid.; Mendoza et al., *Four Great Rivers to Cross*, 57–59.

3. TERMS OF SURRENDER

1. Patricia Kinney Kaufman, *My Mother's People to Colorado They Came*, 33; Reginald S. Craig, *The Fighting Parson: Biography of Colonel John M. Chivington*, 144–46.

2. Craig, *Fighting Parson*, 181.

3. Ibid., 182–83; *Daily Tribune*, October 16, 1971.

4. Craig, *Fighting Parson*, 176.

5. Preston Holder, *Hoe and Horse on the Plains: A Study of Cultural Development among Native American Indians*, 104–5.

6. Ibid.

7. Craig, *Fighting Parson*, 184.

8. *Report of the Secretary of War Sand Creek Massacre*, Senate Document 142, 18–24.

9. *Daily Tribune*, October 16, 1971; *Delphi Weekly Times*, September 8, 1865.

10. Kaufman, *My Mother's People*, 33.

11. Proclamation from Governor Evans to Colonel Chivington and Colonel Chivington to Troops, November 9, 1863.

12. Craig, *Fighting Parson*, 190.

13. Ibid., 182–83; *Chronicles of Oklahoma*.

14. *Chronicles of Oklahoma*; Craig, *Fighting Parson*, 182–83.

15. Craig, *Fighting Parson*, 157–58; Susan Brownmiller, *Against Our Will: Men, Women and Rape*, 140–41.

16. Brownmiller, *Against Our Will*; Jacob P. Dunn, *Massacres of the Mountains*, 219–24.

17. Dunn, *Massacres of the Mountains*, 219–24.

18. *Denver Republican*, May 18, 1890.

19. Ibid.

20. Craig, *Fighting Parson*, 181.

21. Ibid., 186; *Delphi Weekly Times*, September 8, 1865; Patrick Mendoza, *Song of Sorrow: Massacre at Sand Creek*, 88–89.

22. Craig, *Fighting Parson*, 183–84; *Report of the Secretary of War Sand Creek Massacre*, Senate Executive Document 142, 104–5.

23. *Report of the Secretary of War Sand Creek Massacre*, Senate Executive Document 26, 211–12; Craig, *Fighting Parson*, 182; Letter from L. W. Colby to Lt. Colonel Samuel F. Tappan.

24. Craig, *Fighting Parson*, 184; *Report of the Secretary of War Sand Creek Massacre*, Senate Executive Document 142, 29.

25. *Report of the Secretary of War Sand Creek Massacre*, Senate Executive Document 142, 29.

26. Kaufman, *My Mother's People*, 33.

27. Craig, *Fighting Parson*, 184.

28. Ibid., 184–86.

29. Mendoza, *Song of Sorrow*, 88–90.

30. Craig, *Fighting Parson*, 186–87; *Report of the Secretary of War Sand Creek Massacre*, Senate Document 26, 47.

31. *Report of the Secretary of War Sand Creek Massacre*, Senate Document 26, 47; Craig, *Fighting Parson*, 186–87.

32. Kaufman, *My Mother's People*, 33.

33. *Denver Republican*, October 5, 1894; Craig, *Fighting Parson*, 188–89.

34. Ibid.

35. *Delphi Weekly Times*, September 8, 1865; George E. Hyde, *Life of George Bent: Written from His Letters*, 151–53.

36. Hyde, *Life of George Bent*, 151–53; Peter Harrison, *Mochi: Cheyenne Woman Warrior*, 4–5; Patrick M. Mendoza, Ann Strange-Owl-Raben, and Nico Strange-Owl, *Four Great Rivers to Cross: Cheyenne History, Culture and Traditions*, 63–65.

37. Grace Jackson Penney, *Tales of the Cheyennes*, 15–18; George Bird Grinnell, "Some Early Cheyenne Tales," *Journal of American Folklore*.

38. Grinnell, "Some Early Cheyenne Tales"; Penney, *Tales of the Cheyennes*, 16–20.

39. Ibid.

40. Grinnell, "Some Early Cheyenne Tales"; Penney, *Tales of the Cheyennes*, 18–21.

41. Ibid.

42. Grinnell, "Some Early Cheyenne Tales"; Penney, *Tales of the Cheyennes*, 19–23.

43. Ibid.

44. Penney, *Tales of the Cheyennes*, 20–25.

45. Ibid.

46. *Elbert County Banner*, September 1, 1899.

4. NOTHING LIVES LONG

1. *Elbert County Banner*, September 1, 1899; Patricia Kinney Kaufman, *My Mother's People to Colorado They Came*, 33–34; Patrick M. Mendoza, *Song of Sorrow: Massacre at Sand Creek*, 91; Lori Cox-Paul, "John M. Chivington: The 'Reverend Colonel' 'Marry-Your-Daughter' 'Sand Creek Massacre,'" 130.

2. Patrick M. Mendoza, Ann Strange-Owl-Raben, and Nico Strange-Owl, *Four Great Rivers to Cross: Cheyenne History, Culture and Traditions*, 66–68; *Denver Republican*, October 5, 1894; Reginald S. Craig, *The Fighting Parson: Biography of Colonel John M. Chivington*, 188–89.

3. Craig, *Fighting Parson*, 190; Luella Shaw, *True History of Some of the Pioneers of Colorado*, 81.

4. *Delphi Weekly Times*, September 8, 1865; George E. Hyde, *Life of George Bent Written from His Letters*, 144–45.

5. *Daily Tribune*, October 16, 1971; Mendoza, *Song of Sorrow*, 96.

6. Mendoza, *Song of Sorrow*, 97–98; *Delphi Weekly Times*, September 8, 1865.

7. *Delphi Weekly Times*, September 8, 1865; Kaufman, *My Mother's People*, 33; Craig, *Fighting Parson*, 192.

8. *Rocky Mountain News*, January 13, 1865; *Daily Tribune*, October 16, 1971.

9. *Daily Tribune*, October 16, 1971; Hyde, *Life of George Bent*, 155; Mendoza, *Song of Sorrow*, 97.

10. Mendoza, *Song of Sorrow*, 97; *Delphi Weekly Times*, September 8, 1865; Mendoza et al., *Four Great Rivers to Cross*, 69.

11. Mendoza et al., *Four Great Rivers to Cross*, 70; Peter Harrison, *Mochi: Cheyenne Woman Warrior*, 4–5; *Report from the Secretary of War Sand Creek Massacre*, 182; Linda Wommack and John L. Sipes, Jr., "Mo-chi: First Female Cheyenne Warrior," *Wild West Magazine*, April 2008.

12. Craig, *Fighting Parson*, 196; Hyde, *Life of George Bent*, 156.

13. Hyde, *Life of George Bent*, 194; *Rocky Mountain News*, January 13, 1865; *Rocky Mountain News*, March 3, 1929.

14. Craig, *Fighting Parson*, 196; Kaufman, *My Mother's People*, 34; *Dubois County Daily Herald*, March 23, 1973; *Huntington Democrat*, August 31, 1863.

15. Hyde, *Life of George Bent*, 157–58.

16. *Daily Missouri Republican*, August 18, 1865.

17. *Delphi Weekly Times*, September 8, 1865.

18. *Rocky Mountain News*, December 22, 1864.

19. Eugene Ware, *The Indian Wars of 1864*, 280–85.

20. *Miners Register*, November 11, 1869.

21. Craig, *Fighting Parson*, 202; Kaufman, *My Mother's People*, 34–35.

22. Cox-Paul, "John M. Chivington: The 'Reverend Colonel,'" 132; Kaufman, *My Mother's People*, 35.

23. Kaufman, *My Mother's People*, 35; Joseph Cummins, *The World's Bloodiest History*, 99.

24. Jacob P. Dunn, *Massacres of the Mountains*, 427; *Report of the Secretary of War Sand Creek Massacre*, Senate Document 142.

25. *Report of the Secretary of War Sand Creek Massacre*, Senate Document 142; Craig, *Fighting Parson*, 261–64.

26. Craig, *Fighting Parson*, 264–65; *Report of the Secretary of War Sand Creek Massacre*, Senate Document 142.

27. U.S. Senate Documents, Reports of Committee No. 156; Craig, *Fighting Parson*, 205; Hyde, *Life of George Bent*, 163.

28. Hyde, *Life of George Bent*, 169–70; Craig, *Fighting Parson*, 221; Harrison, *Mochi: Cheyenne Woman Warrior*, 4; Wommack and Sipes, "Mo-chi: First Female Cheyenne Warrior."

29. Wommack and Sipes, "Mo-chi: First Female Cheyenne Warrior"; Mendoza et al., *Four Great Rivers to Cross*, 70–71.

30. George Bird Grinnell, *The Cheyenne Indians: Their History & Lifeways*, 193–94.

31. Ibid.

32. Mendoza et al., *Four Rivers to Cross*, 75; Harrison, *Mochi: Cheyenne Woman Warrior*, 4.

33. Craig, *Fighting Parson*, 264–65; *Report of the Secretary of War Sand Creek Massacre*, Senate Document 142.

34. *Report of the Secretary of War Sand Creek Massacre*, Senate Document 142.

35. Grinnell, *Cheyenne Indians*, 193–94; Hyde, *Life of George Bent*, 200–1.

36. Harrison, *Mochi: Cheyenne Woman Warrior*, 4; Mendoza et al., *Four Rivers to Cross*, 74–75.

5. THE MISSING

1. Patrick M. Mendoza, Ann Strange-Owl-Raben, and Nico Strange-Owl, *Four Great Rivers to Cross: Cheyenne History, Culture and Traditions*, 61, 74–75; Grace Jackson Penney, *Tales of the Cheyennes*, 2–4.

2. Penney, *Tales of the Cheyennes*, 2–4; George Bird Grinnell, *The Cheyenne Indians: Their History & Lifeways*, 202–3.

3. Grinnell, *Cheyenne Indians*, 202–3; *Report of the Secretary of War Sand Creek Massacre*, 182; George E. Hyde, *Life of George Bent Written from His Letters*, 241–43.

4. Hyde, *Life of George Bent*, 200–201; Patrick M. Mendoza, *Song of Sorrow: Massacre at Sand Creek*, 106; Peter Harrison, *Mochi: Cheyenne Woman Warrior*, 4; *Galveston Daily Bulletin*, December 1, 1868; Linda Wommack and John L. Sipes, Jr., "Mo-chi: First Female Cheyenne Warrior," *Wild West Magazine*, April 2008.

5. Wommack and Sipes, "Mo-chi: First Female Cheyenne Warrior"; Hyde, *Life of George Bent*, 164–68.

6. Hyde, *Life of George Bent*, 132, 177; *New York Times*, July 23, 1865.

7. Hyde, *Life of George Bent*, 178; Mendoza, *Song of Sorrow*, 131.

8. *Galveston Daily Bulletin*, December 1, 1868.

9. *Galveston Daily News*, August 9, 1886.

10. Mendoza, *Song of Sorrow*, 110–11, 128.

11. Hyde, *Life of George Bent*, 178–82.

12. Ibid.; Mendoza et al., *Four Great Rivers to Cross*, 75.

13. Mendoza, *Song of Sorrow*, 110–11; *Galveston Daily News*, August 9, 1886.

14. *Galveston Daily Bulletin*, December 1, 1868.

15. Mendoza, *Song of Sorrow*, 144; Wommack and Sipes, "Mo-chi: First Female Cheyenne Warrior," http://home.epix.net~landis/mochi.html as prepared by John L. Sipes; Harrison, *Mochi: Cheyenne Woman Warrior*, 4; Mendoza et al., *Four Great Rivers to Cross*, 75; *Emporia Daily Gazette*, April 13, 1925.

16. *Emporia Daily Gazette*, April 13, 1925; *Hutchinson News*, July 16, 1972; Hyde, *Life of George Bent*, 246–49.

17. Hyde, *Life of George Bent*, 248; *Hutchinson News*, July 16, 1972; Harrison, *Mochi: Cheyenne Woman Warrior*, 5; Mendoza et al., *Four Great Rivers to Cross*, 75.

18. *San Antonio Light*, August 17, 1972; Hyde, *Life of George Bent*, 283–84; *Blockton News*, October 7, 1937.

19. *New Albany Daily Leader*, October 31, 1867.

20. *Blockton News*, October 7, 1937; Hyde, *Life of George Bent*, 248.

21. Hyde, *Life of George Bent*, 248–49.

22. *Report of the Secretary of War Sand Creek Massacre*, 25–31; Harrison, *Mochi: Cheyenne Woman Warrior*, 6.

23. Grinnell, *Fighting Cheyennes*, 254–58.

24. Ibid.; *Blockton News*, October 7, 1937; Hyde, *Life of George Bent*, 298–99; *New Albany Leader*, October 31, 1867.

25. Mendoza et al., *Four Great Rivers to Cross*, 75; Harrison, *Mochi: Cheyenne Woman Warrior*, 5.

26. Jerome Greene, *Washita: The U.S. Army and the Southern Cheyenne 1867–1869*, 103–8; Barbara Andre, "Custer at the Washita," *West Magazine*, June 1968; Mendoza, *Song of Sorrow*, 138–39.

27. Mendoza, *Song of Sorrow*, 138–39; Greene, *Washita*, 103–8; Andre, "Custer at the Washita."

28. *Indianapolis Journal*, June 29, 1869.

29. Harrison, *Mochi: Cheyenne Woman Warrior*, 5; Wommack and Sipes, "Mo-chi: First Female Cheyenne Warrior."

30. Ibid.

6. LESSONS FROM YELLOW-HAIRED WOMAN

1. *Indianapolis Daily Journal*, June 29, 1869; Barbara Andre, "Custer at the Washita," *West Magazine*, June 1968; *Daily Rocky Mountain News*, December 29, 1868.

2. George Custer, "Report on the Battle of Washita," November 28, 1868.

3. *Daily Rocky Mountain News*, December 29, 1868.

4. *Blockton News*, October 7, 1937; Patrick M. Mendoza, *Song of Sorrow: Massacre at Sand Creek*, 138–39; Jerome Greene, *Washita: The U.S. Army and the Southern Cheyennes, 1867–1869*, 103–6; George E. Hyde, *Life of George Bent Written from His Letters*, 293, 296–97; Peter Harrison, *Mochi: Cheyenne Woman Warrior*, 5–6.

5. Custer, "Report on the Battle of Washita."

6. Patrick M. Mendoza, Ann Strange-Owl-Raben, and Nico Strange-Owl, *Four Great Rivers to Cross: Cheyenne History, Culture and Traditions*, 75; Linda Wommack and John L. Sipes, Jr., "Mo-chi: First Female Cheyenne Warrior," *Wild West Magazine*, April 2008; Harrison, *Mochi: Cheyenne Woman Warrior*, 5–6.

7. Harrison, *Mochi: Cheyenne Woman Warrior*, 5–6; Hyde, *Life of George Bent*, 22–24; Richard S. Grimes, "Cheyenne Dog Soldiers," www.manataka.org; Mendoza et al., *Four Great Rivers to Cross*, 57.

8. Mendoza et al., *Four Great Rivers to Cross*, 57; Bryce Walker, *Through Indian Eyes: The Untold Story of Native American Peoples*, 207; *Belleville Daily Freeman*, May 24, 1905.

9. Wommack and Sipes, "Mo-chi: First Female Cheyenne Warrior"; Harrison, *Mochi: Cheyenne Woman Warrior*, 5–6.

10. John Speer, "Report to Fred Martin of Interview with Mrs. J. M. Chivington"; Reginald S. Craig, *The Fighting Parson: Biography of Colonel John M. Chivington*, 232–33.

11. Craig, *Fighting Parson*, 232–33; Lori Cox-Paul, "John M. Chivington: The 'Reverend Colonel' 'Marry-Your-Daughter' 'Sand Creek Massacre,'" *Nebraska History* 88, 132–34.

12. Cox-Paul, "John M. Chivington: The 'Reverend Colonel,'" 132–34; Craig, *Fighting Parson*, 232–34; Speer, "Report to Fred Martin."

13. Patricia Kinney Kaufman, *My Mother's People to Colorado They Came*, 34–35; Cox-Paul, "John M. Chivington: The 'Reverend Colonel,'" 134–35.

14. *Sullivan Democrat*, November 1, 1866; *Denver Republican*, October 5, 1894.

15. Kaufman, *My Mother's People*, 34–35; Cox-Paul, "John M. Chivington: The 'Reverend Colonel,'" 134–35.

16. *Columbus Daily Telegram*, August 8, 1969; Hyde, *Life of George Bent*, 200–4.

17. Hyde, *Life of George Bent*, 329–31; George Bird Grinnell, *The Fighting Cheyennes*, 316–18; Harrison, *Mochi: Cheyenne Woman Warrior*, 6.

18. Harrison, *Mochi: Cheyenne Woman Warrior*, 6; *Janesville Gazette*, April 8, 1873.

19. Ibid.

20. Ibid.

21. Mendoza et al., *Four Great Rivers to Cross*, 99–100; Hyde, *Life of George Bent*, 355–56.

22. *Anglo American Times*, August 8, 1874.

23. Mendoza et al., *Four Great Rivers to Cross*, 75; Harrison, *Mochi: Cheyenne Woman Warrior*, 6–7.

24. Harrison, *Mochi: Cheyenne Woman Warrior*, 6–7; Mendoza et al., *Four Great Rivers to Cross*, 75; Mendoza, *Song of Sorrow*, 144–46.

7. SAVAGE AND CRUEL

1. Peter Harrison, *Mochi: Cheyenne Woman Warrior*, 7; Patrick M. Mendoza, *Song of Sorrow: Massacre at Sand Creek*, 144; Patrick M. Mendoza, Ann Strange-Owl-Raben, and Nico Strange-Owl, *Four Great Rivers to Cross: Chey-

enne History, Culture and Traditions, 75; Linda Wommack and John L. Sipes, Jr., "Mo-chi: First Female Cheyenne Warrior," *Wild West Magazine*, April 2008.

2. George E. Hyde, *Life of George Bent Written from His Letters*, 360–61; Peter Harrison, *Mochi: Cheyenne Woman Warrior*, 7; Patrick M. Mendoza, *Song of Sorrow: Massacre at Sand Creek*, 143–44.

3. T. G. McGee, *Echoes of Eighty-Nine*, 129.

4. *Chronicles of Oklahoma*, 292–98, www.hennessey.lib.ok.us/who-killed.htm.

5. Letter from Agent J. D. Miles to the Office of Indian Affairs in Washington, July 10, 1874.

6. *Chronicles of Oklahoma*, 292–98; Harrison, *Mochi: Cheyenne Woman Warrior*, 8–9.

7. Mendoza, *Song of Sorrow*, 144; Hyde, *Life of George Bent*, 360–61.

8. F. C. Montgomery, "Lone Tree, Meade County United States Surveyors Massacred by Indians," *Kansas Historical Quarterly* 1, no. 3 (May 1932), 266; *Lawrence Journal World*, May 4, 1933; *Lawrence Journal World*, March 21, 1935.

9. *Lawrence Journal World*, March 21, 1935; *Lawrence Journal World*, May 4, 1933; Montgomery, "Lone Tree, Meade County," 266.

10. Montgomery, "Lone Tree, Meade County," 266; Harrison, *Mochi: Cheyenne Woman Warrior*, 9; *Lawrence Journal World*, March 21, 1935.

11. *Lawrence Journal World*, March 21, 1935; Montgomery, "Lone Tree, Meade County," 266.

12. *Atchison Globe*, September 6, 1874.

13. Montgomery, "Lone Tree, Meade County," 266.

14. Harrison, *Mochi: Cheyenne Woman Warrior*, 9; Mendoza et al., *Four Great Rivers to Cross*, 75; Hyde, *Life of George Bent*, 361–63.

15. *Greencastle Star*, February 22, 1879.

16. Ibid.

17. John Speer, "Report to Fred Martin of Interview with Mrs. J. M. Chivington."

18. Ibid.; Patricia Kinney Kaufman, *My Mother's People to Colorado They Came*, 35; Reginald S. Craig, *The Fighting Parson: Biography of Colonel John M. Chivington*, 234–35.

19. *Petersburg Index-Appeal*, June 13, 1868.

20. Ibid.; Kaufman, *My Mother's People*, 35.

21. Craig, *Fighting Parson*, 233–34; Speer, "Report to Fred Martin."

22. Lori Cox-Paul, "John M. Chivington: The 'Reverend Colonel' 'Marry-Your-Daughter' 'Sand Creek Massacre,'" *Nebraska History* 88; *The Press*, March 12, 1875.

23. *Clinton County Democrat*, August 15, 1881; Speer, "Report to Fred Martin."

24. Speer, "Report to Fred Martin"; *Clinton County Democrat*, August 15, 1881.

25. *Morning Oregonian*, July 25, 1862; *Indianapolis Daily Journal*, June 15, 1867.

26. Harrison, *Mochi: Cheyenne Woman Warrior*, 8–9; Mendoza et al., *Four Great Rivers to Cross*, 75.

27. Mendoza et al., *Four Great Rivers to Cross*, 75; Harrison, *Mochi: Cheyenne Woman Warrior*, 8–9; Mendoza, *Song of Sorrow*, 144–45.

8. MOCHI

1. Grace E. Meredith, *Girl Captives of the Cheyennes: A True Story of the Capture and Rescue of Four Pioneer Girls, 1874*, 17–20; Peter Harrison, *Mochi: Cheyenne Woman Warrior*, 9–10.

2. Harrison, *Mochi: Cheyenne Woman Warrior*, 9–10; Patrick M. Mendoza, Ann Strange-Owl-Raben, and Nico Strange-Owl, *Four Great Rivers to Cross: Cheyenne History, Culture and Traditions*, 75; Meredith, *Girl Captives of the Cheyennes*, 17–20.

3. Ibid.

4. Ibid.

5. Ibid.

6. Ibid.

7. Harrison, *Mochi: Cheyenne Woman Warrior*, 9–10; Meredith, *Girl Captives of the Cheyennes*, 23–26.

8. Meredith, *Girl Captives of the Cheyennes*, 23–26; Harrison, *Mochi: Cheyenne Woman Warrior*, 10–13.

9. Harrison, *Mochi: Cheyenne Woman Warrior*, 10–13; Meredith, *Girl Captives of the Cheyennes*, 20–21.

10. Meredith, *Girl Captives of the Cheyennes*, 20–21.

11. *Neosho Valley Register*, December 12, 1874; Harrison, *Mochi: Cheyenne Woman Warrior*, 11–13.

12. Harrison, *Mochi: Cheyenne Woman Warrior*, 11–13; Meredith, *Girl Captives of the Cheyennes*, 25–29; *Neosho Valley Register*, December 12, 1874.

13. Meredith, *Girl Captives of the Cheyennes*, 25–29.

14. Ibid., 31.

15. Ibid., 29–30; *Neosho Valley Register*, December 12, 1874.

16. Meredith, *Girl Captives of the Cheyennes*, 57–59.

17. *Neosho Valley Register*, December 12, 1874.

18. Mendoza et al., *Four Great Rivers to Cross*, 75–76; Harrison, *Mochi: Cheyenne Woman Warrior*, 13–15.

19. Harrison, *Mochi: Cheyenne Woman Warrior*, 13–15; George E. Hyde, *Life of George Bent Written from His Letters*, 361–62; Patrick M. Mendoza, *Song of Sorrow: Massacre at Sand Creek*, 146.

20. Meredith, *Girl Captives of the Cheyennes*, 56–58.

21. *Hagerstown Herald & Torch Light*, December 2, 1874; Hyde, *Life of George Bent*, 363–65; Meredith, *Girl Captives of the Cheyennes*, 70–71.

22. Meredith, *Girl Captives of the Cheyennes*, 70–71.

23. Ibid., 71–72.

24. Hyde, *Life of George Bent*, 363–65; *Hagerstown Herald & Torch Light*, December 2, 1874; Harrison, *Mochi: Cheyenne Woman Warrior*, 14–17.

25. Harrison, *Mochi: Cheyenne Woman Warrior*, 14–17; Meredith, *Girl Captives of the Cheyennes*, 86–87.

26. Meredith, *Girl Captives of the Cheyennes*, 89–90.

27. Harrison, *Mochi: Cheyenne Woman Warrior*, 14–17; Hyde, *Life of George Bent*, 364.

28. Harrison, *Mochi: Cheyenne Woman Warrior*, 18–19; Mendoza et al., *Four Great Rivers to Cross*, 75; Linda Wommack and John L. Sipes, Jr., "Mochi: First Female Cheyenne Warrior," *Wild West Magazine*, April 2008.

9. LIFE AT FORT MARION

1. *Nesho Valley Register*, December 12, 1874; Peter Harrison, *Mochi: Cheyenne Woman Warrior*, 16–17.

2. Patrick M. Mendoza, Ann Strange-Owl-Raben, and Nico Strange-Owl, *Four Great Rivers to Cross: Cheyenne History, Culture and Traditions*, 102–3; Grace E. Meredith, *Girl Captives of the Cheyennes: A True Story of the Capture and Rescue of Four Pioneer Girls, 1874*, 108–9; Brad D. Lookingbill, *War Dance at Fort Marion: Plains Indian War Prisoners*, 85.

3. Lookingbill, *War Dance at Fort Marion*, 85; Mendoza et al., *Four Great Rivers to Cross*, 102–3.

4. Meredith, *Girl Captives of the Cheyennes*, 25–29; Harrison, *Mochi: Cheyenne Woman Warrior*, 24.

5. Harrison, *Mochi: Cheyenne Woman Warrior*, 24; Lookingbill, *War Dance at Fort Marion*, 31–32.

6. Patrick M. Mendoza, *Song of Sorrow: Massacre at Sand Creek*, 147; Mendoza et al., *Four Great Rivers to Cross*, 103.

7. *Greencastle Banner*, August 5, 1875; *The Press*, May 26, 1875; Lookingbill, *War Dance at Fort Marion*, 54–55.

8. *Athens Post*, May 23, 1875.

9. *Greencastle Banner*, August 5, 1875.

10. Harrison, *Mochi: Cheyenne Woman Warrior*, 26–27.

11. *Florida Press*, July 3, 1875; *Billings Gazette*, October 22, 1933; Lookingbill, *War Dance at Fort Marion*, 59–60.

12. Lookingbill, *War Dance at Fort Marion*, 63–64.

13. Ibid., 66–69.

14. Ibid., 67; Memorandum on Sending Indian Prisoners to Fort Marion.

15. Ibid..

16. Mendoza et al., *Four Great Rivers to Cross*, 102; *Sallisaw Star*, September 11, 1908.

17. Lookingbill, *War Dance at Fort Marion*, 77.

18. Ibid., 5–6, 78–80.

19. Ibid., 112.

20. Ibid., 85, 95; *Salt Lake Tribune*, March 22, 1936.

21. *Dubuque Herald*, August 15, 1875; Harrison, *Mochi: Cheyenne Woman Warrior*, 27.

22. Lookingbill, *War Dance at Fort Marion*, 122–23.

23. *Athens Messenger*, January 25, 1877.

24. Ibid.; Lookingbill, *War Dance at Fort Marion*, 125.

25. *Indianapolis Journal*, October 30, 1875.

26. Lookingbill, *War Dance at Fort Marion*, 96, 112–13.

27. John Speer, "Report to Fred Martin of Interview with Mrs. John Chivington"; Reginald S. Craig, *The Fighting Parson: Biography of Colonel John M. Chivington*, 233–34; Patricia Kinney Kaufman, *My Mother's People to Colorado They Came*, 36–37.

28. *Lebanon Patriot*, August 24, 1883.

29. *Clinton County Democrat*, August 17, 1883.

30. *Daily Denver Times*, October 8, 1883.

31. Ibid.; Kaufman, *My Mother's People*, 36; Craig, *Fighting Parson*, 233.

32. Craig, *Fighting Parson*, 234–35; *Daily Denver Times*, October 8, 1883.

33. Ibid.

34. Harrison, *Mochi: Cheyenne Woman Warrior*, 28; Mendoza et al., *Four Great Rivers to Cross*, 102–3; Linda Wommack and John L. Sipes, Jr., "Mo-chi: First Female Cheyenne Warrior," *Wild West Magazine* April 2008; Mendoza, *Song of Sorrow*, 164; Lookingbill, *War Dance at Fort Marion*, 95.

10. NEVER TO BE HOME AGAIN

1. *Daily Graphic*, April 26, 1878; Brad D. Lookingbill, *War Dance at Fort Marion: Plains Indian War Prisoners*, 85–88, 94–95.

2. Lookingbill, *War Dance at Fort Marion*, 87; *New Smyrna Daily News*, December 3, 1915; *Aurora Dearborn Independent* April 15, 1880.

3. Lookingbill, *War Dance at Fort Marion*, 87–89.

4. Ibid., 57, 65–66; George Bird Grinnell, *The Fighting Cheyennes*, 132–34.

5. Lookingbill, *War Dance at Fort Marion*, 67–68.

6. Ibid., 159–60, 245.

7. *Indianapolis Journal*, April 17, 1878; Peter Harrison, *Mochi: Cheyenne Woman Warrior*, 27–28; Patrick M. Mendoza, *Song of Sorrow: Massacre at Sand Creek*, 164.

8. *Indianapolis Journal*, April 19, 1878.

9. Lookingbill, *War Dance at Fort Marion*, 178–79; "Pathetic Letter from Indians," *Southern Workman*, June 8, 1879, 68.

10. *Indianapolis Journal*, October 20, 1878.

11. *Petersburg Index-Appeal*, April 30, 1878; *Galveston Daily News*, May 1, 1878; *Dearborn County Register*, April 15, 1880; *Elkhart Sentinel*, July 31, 1885; *Reno Evening Gazette*, December 3, 1889.

12. Biren Bonnerjea, *Reminiscences of a Cheyenne*, 9–11; George Bird Grinnell, *The Cheyenne Indians: Their History & Lifeways*, 193.

13. Harrison, *Mochi: Cheyenne Woman Warrior*, 28; Linda Wommack and John L. Sipes, Jr., "Mo-chi: First Female Cheyenne Warrior," *Wild West Magazine*, April 2008; Mendoza, *Song of Sorrow*, 164.

14. Mendoza, *Song of Sorrow*, 164; Wommack and Sipes, "Mo-chi: First Female Cheyenne Warrior."

EPILOGUE

1. Patrick M. Mendoza, Ann Strange-Owl-Raben, and Nico Strange-Owl, *Four Great Rivers to Cross: Cheyenne History, Culture and Traditions*, 36–37; John Speer, "Report to Fred Martin of Interview with Mrs. John M. Chivington"; Reginald S. Craig, *The Fighting Parson: Biography of Colonel John M. Chivington*, 236–37.

2. Speer, "Report to Fred Martin"; Craig, *Fighting Parson*, 236–37.

3. Ibid.

4. Ibid.

5. *American Register*, November 3, 1894.

6. Patrick M. Mendoza, *Song of Sorrow: Sand Creek Massacre*, 163; *Sante Fe Reporter*, December 14–20, 1988; Grace E. Meredith, *Girl Captives of the Cheyennes: A True Story of the Capture and Rescue of Four Pioneer Girls, 1874*, 104–12.

7. Meredith, *Girl Captives of the Cheyennes*, 104-12; *Lawrence Republican Daily*, October 1, 1875.

8. *Pampa News*, March 7, 1943; Meredith, *Girl Captives of the Cheyennes*, 104–12.

9. Meredith, *Girl Captives of the Cheyennes*, 112–13; *Lima Sunday News*, August 8, 1926.

10. *Daily News*, May 16, 1925.

11. *Salt Lake Tribune*, March 22, 1936; Richard Henry Pratt, www.arlingtoncemetery.net.

12. Ibid.

13. Brad D. Lookingbill, *War Dance at Fort Marion: Plains Indian War Prisoners*, 201–2.

14. *Colorado Springs Gazette*, May 28, 1999; *Farmington Daily Times*; February 21, 1999.

REMEMBERING SAND CREEK

1. *Medicine Hat News*, March 12, 1991.
2. John Stands in Timber and Margot Liberty, *A Cheyenne Voice*.
3. *Sand Creek Massacre Project Site Location Study*.

BIBLIOGRAPHY

Andre, Barbara. "Custer at the Washita," *West Magazine* 9, no. 1 (June 1968).

Beardsley, Isaac H. *Echoes from Peak and Plain: Tales of Life, War, Travel, and Colorado Methodism*. Cincinnati: Curts & Jennings and New York: Eaton and Mains, 1898.

Bonnerjea, Biren. *Reminiscences of a Cheyenne*. 1935.

Brownmiller, Susan. *Against Our Will: Men, Women and Rape*. New York: Ballantine Books, 1993.

Chivington, John M. *Deposition and Synopsis of the Sand Creek Investigation*. Colorado Historical Society: Denver, June 1865.

Cox-Paul, Lori. "John M. Chivington: The 'Reverend Colonel' 'Marry-Your-Daughter' 'Sand Creek Massacre.'" *Nebraska History* 88 (2007).

Craig, Reginald S. *The Fighting Parson: Biography of Colonel John M. Chivington*. Los Angeles: Westernlore Press, 1959.

Cummins, Joseph. *The World's Bloodiest History*. London: Fair Winds Press, 2009.

Custer, George. "Report on the Battle of Washita." November 28, 1868.

Davis, Athis Sale. "Annette Blackburn Ehler and the Pat Hennessey Memorial Garden." *Chronicles of Oklahoma*, Oklahoma City, 1937.

Documents on the Sand Creek Massacre. www.pbs.org/weta/thewest/resources/archives. Accessed October 27, 2014.

"Dog Soldiers." www.pbs.org/weta/thewest/program/episodes. Accessed October 27, 2014.

"Desire to Punish the Cheyenne Indians." www.accessgenealogy.com/native/desire-punish-cheyenne-indians.htm. Accessed October 27, 2014.

Dunn, Jacob P. *Massacres of the Mountains*. New York: Harper & Brothers, 1880.

Ellenbecker, John G. *The Little Blue River Tragedy: The Captivity of Lucinda Eubank and Laura Roper at the Oak Grove Massacre*. Niwot, CO: Prairie Lake Publisher, 1993.

————. "Oak Grove Massacre, Indian Raids on the Little Blue River." *Marysville Advocate Democrat* 42, no. 16 (1927).

Gibson, Arrell Morgan. "St. Augustine Prisoners." *Red River Valley Historical Review* 3, Fargo, ND (1978).

"Great Indian Battle." http://freepages.genealogy.rootsweb.ancestry.com/~wynkoop/webdocs/1231868.htm. Accessed October 27, 2014.

Greene, Jerome. *Washita: The U.S. Army and the Southern Cheyenne 1867–1869*. Norman: University of Oklahoma Press, 2004.

Grimes, Richard S. "Cheyenne Dog Soldiers." www.manataka.org/page164.html. Accessed October 27, 2014.

Grinnell, George Bird. *The Cheyenne Indians: Their History & Lifeways*. Bloomington, IN: Library of Perennial Philosophy, 2008.

————. *The Fighting Cheyennes*. New York: Charles Scribner's Sons, 1915.

————. "Some Early Cheyenne Tales." *Journal of American Folklore* 20, nos. 78 and 82 (July–September 1907), Southwest Museum Library, Los Angeles.

Harrison, Peter. *Mochi: Cheyenne Woman Warrior*. London: Western Publications, 2009.

History of the Reverends John M. and Isaac Chivington in their Relationship to the Early Methodist Episcopal Church in Kansas and Nebraska. Denver Public Library.

Hyde, George E. *Life of George Bent Written from His Letters*. Norman: University of Oklahoma, 1968.

"Indian Commission on Sand Creek." http://freepages.genealogy.rootsweb.ancestry.com/~wynkoop/webdocs/1221868a.htm. Accessed October 27, 2014.

"Indian Wars: The Battle of Washita, 1868." www.gilderlehrman.org /history-by-era/development-west/resources/indian-wars-battle-washita-1868. Accessed October 27, 2014.

"Interview with Mrs. Chivington about John Chivington, Her Husband." Kansas Historical Society handwritten document dated March 11, 1902.

Kaufman, Patricia Kinney. *My Mother's People to Colorado They Came*. Portland, OR: Paddlewheel Press Publishers, 1994.

Kelley, C. Brian. *Best Little Stories from the Wild West*. Nashville, TN: Cumberland House, 2002.

Leasure, Virginia N. "The Captivity of Laura L. Roper." Unpublished manuscript in Nebraska State Historical Society. Lincoln, Nebraska, January 20, 1974.

Letter from Agent J. D. Miles to the Office of Indian Affairs in Washington, July 10, 1874.

Letter from John M. Chivington to Reverend Fisher. June 23, 1863.

Letter from General L. W. Colby to S. F. Tappan re: Sand Creek Massacre. January 18, 1892.

Lookingbill, Brad D. *War Dance at Fort Marion: Plains Indian War Prisoners*. Norman: University of Oklahoma Press, 2006.

Lowie, Robert H. *Indians of the Plains*. Lincoln, NE: Bison Books, 1982.

McGee, T. G. *Echoes of Eighty-Nine*. Kingfisher, OK: Kingfisher Times & Free Press, 1939.

Mellor, Wm. J. "The Military Investigation of Colonel J. M. Chivington," *Chronicles of Oklahoma* 16, no. 4 (December 1938).

Memorandum on Sending Indian Prisoners to Fort Marion, Roll 45, M565.

Mendoza, Patrick M., Ann Strange-Owl-Raben, and Nico Strange-Owl. *Four Great Rivers to Cross: Cheyenne History, Culture and Traditions*. Englewood, CO: Teachers Idea Press, 1998.

Mendoza, Patrick M. *Song of Sorrow: Massacre at Sand Creek*. Denver, CO: Willow Wind Publishing, 1993.

Meredith, Grace E. *Girl Captives of the Cheyennes: A True Story of the Capture and Rescue of Four Pioneer Girls, 1874*. Los Angeles: Gem Publishing Company, 1927.

Monnett, John H. *Massacre at Cheyenne Hole; Lt. Austin Henely and the Sappa Creek Company*. Boulder: University of Colorado, 1999.

Montgomery, F. C. "Lone Tree, Meade County United States Surveyors Massacred by Indians." *Kansas Historical Quarterly* 1, no. 3 (May 1932).

"More of Custer and Black Kettle." http://freepages.genealogy.rootsweb.ancestry.com/~wynkoop /webdocs/12231868.htm. Accessed October 27, 2014.

"Mrs. Isabella Chivington." *Trail Magazine* 3, no. 6 (November 1910), Denver, Colorado.

OK-Lawmen-Outlaw-L Archives: The Murder of Patrick Hennessey. http:// archiver.rootsweb.ancestry.com/th/read/OK-Lawmen-Outlaw. Accessed October 27, 2014.

Orders from John M. Chivington to Asst. Adjutant General. November 9, 1863.

"Pathetic Letter from Indians." *Southern Workman*, June 8, 1879.

Patrick Hennessy. www.hennessey.lib.ok.us/pat_hennessey. Accessed 10/27/2014.

Penney, Grace Jackson. *Tales of the Cheyennes*. Boston, MA: Houghton Mifflin Company, 1953.

Preston, Holder. *The Hoe and Horse on the Plains: A Study of Cultural Development among Native American Indians*. Lincoln: University of Nebraska Press, 1970.

Proclamation from Governor Evans to Colonel Chivington and Colonel Chivington to Troops, November 9, 1863.

Report of the Secretary of War Sand Creek Massacre, Senate Executive Doc. No. 26, 2nd Session. Washington Government Printing Office, 1867.

Report of the Secretary of War Sand Creek Massacre, Senate Executive Doc. No. 142, 2nd Session. Washington Government Printing Office, 1867.

Richard Henry Pratt. www.arlingtoncemetery.net/rhpratt.htm. Accessed October 27, 2014.

Ruth Adams and Joseph Eubank. www.genforum.genealogy.com. Accessed October 27, 2014.

Sand Creek Massacre. www.kclonewolf.com/history/SandCreek/sc-index.html. Accessed October 27, 2014.

Sand Creek Massacre. www.digitalhistory.uh.edu/disp_textbook.cfm?smtID=3&psid=4015. Accessed October 27, 2014.

"Sand Creek Massacre: The Families' Stories." home.epix.net/~landis/sandcreek.html. Accessed October 27, 2014.

Sand Creek Massacre Project Site Location Study. Volume 1, Denver: National Park Service, Intermountain Region, 2001.

Shaw, Luella. *True History of Some of the Pioneers of Colorado*. Hotchkiss, CO: W. S. Coburn, John Patterson and A. K. Shaw, 1909.

Sipes, John L. "Mochi." http://home.epix.net/~landis/mochi.html. Accessed October 27, 2014.

Speer, John. "Report to Fred Martin of Interview with Mrs. John M. Chivington." Manuscript on file in Library of Kansas State Historical Society, Topeka, March 11, 1902.

Stands in Timber, John, and Margo Liberty. *A Cheyenne Voice*. 2nd edition. New Haven, CT: Yale University Press, 1998.

"Statement of Mrs. Ewbanks." http://freepages.genealogy.rootsweb.ancestry.com/~wynkoop/webdocs/9131865a.htm. Accessed October 27, 2014.

Swanton, John R. *Indian Tribes of North America Bulletin*. Baltimore, MD: Smithsonian Institute Bureau of American Ethnology Genealogical Publishing Company, 2003.

Taylor, Joe F. *The Indian Campaign of the Staked Plains 1874–1875*. Military Correspondence from the War Department, Adjutant General's Office, File 2815-1874.

"The Treatment of Women by Indians." *Plain Tales of the Plains from the Trail*. Vol. 8, no. 12 (1916), Nebraska Historical Society, Lincoln, Nebraska.

Vine, Robert, and John Mack Faragher. *The American West: A New Interpretive History*. New Haven, CT: Yale University, 2000.

Walker, Bryce. *Through Indian Eyes: The Untold Story of Native American Peoples*. Louisville, KY: Reader's Digest Association, 1995.

Ware, Eugene. *The Indian Wars of 1864*. London: Dodo Press, 2009.

"Washita and Sand Creek Compared." http://freepages.genealogy.rootsweb.ancestry.com/~wynkoop/webdocs/12291868a.htm. Accessed October 27, 2014.

Wommack, Linda, and John L. Sipes, Jr. "Mo-chi: First Female Cheyenne Warrior." *Wild West Magazine*, April 2008.

INDEX

Blacklidge, Frank, 68–70
Blanche White Shield, 120
blind man, 124–126
"Bloodless Third," xii, 10–11, 25, 35
Bowstring Society, 59–60, 62, 65, 67, 85,
  92–93, 124; Army ordered to capture,
  70; German family attacked by, 77–78;
  government land surveyors killed by,
  63–65; prisoner adaptations of, 96;
  surrender of, 89; surveyors as
  encroaching on lands of, 75
Brady, Ray, 126
Brule, 5
buffalo, 9, 14, 30, 31, 33, 89; Battle of
  Washita and, 53, 59; destruction of, 5,
  50, 51, 59; Plains Indians' dance
  showing importance of, 103
Buffalo Spring Station attack, 67–68
Bull Bear (chief of Dog Soldiers), 22–23

Caloway, Thomas, 67–68
camp crier, 128
Camp Weld, 22–23
Carlisle Indian Industrial School, 100, 115
Castillo de San Marco. See Fort Marion
  prison
Cavalry, U.S., 10. See also "Bloodless
  Third"; Colorado Volunteers; First
  Colorado Volunteer Cavalry Regiment;
  Seventh U.S. Cavalry; Third Colorado
  Cavalry; volunteers
Central Pacific Railroad, 59
chastity, 4
Cheyenne, xi, xii, 2, 5, 8–9, 20, 109–110;
  Adobe Wall attack and, 65; as Battle of
  Washita survivors, 58; as becoming
  unfriendly, 71; breaking free songs by
  women of, 92; Buffalo Spring Station's
  nearby attack of, 67–68; Fort Wise
  treaty with Arapaho and, 9–10; as
  friendliest among Plains Indians, 70;
  German Family attacked by, 77–78;
  German girls as surviving capture by,
  85, 86, 87–89, 91, 114–115; Heap of
  Birds (Cheyenne leader), 105;
  legendary times of, 118; Little Robe
  (Cheyenne chief), 60; marriage
  ceremony customs of, 4; Medicine
  Lodge Creek treaty reservations and,

58, 65; military societies of, 124;
  promised provisions not given to,
  106–107; removal of tribesman refused
  by chiefs of, 95; renegade reputation of
  Mochi and Medicine Water, xiv; roles
  of women as, 14–15; Sand Creek camp
  of, 11; Sand Creek Massacre and
  bravery of, 37; settler disruptions and
  blood raids by, 10–11; as settling in
  Sand Creek, 11, 23; Southern, xiv;
  surrendering bands of, 88, 89; Washita
  land boundary misunderstanding and,
  53; White Antelope (Cheyenne chief),
  22–23, 30, 37, 118, 120, 123. See also
  Black Kettle (Cheyenne chief)
Cheyenne Dog Soldiers. See Dog Soldiers
Cheyenne Mission School, 89
Chicago railroad strike, 115
children, 37, 39–40, 121, 124, 125,
  126–127, 128
Chisholm Trail, 67–68
Chivington, Isaac, 15–16, 20
Chivington, Isabella, 72, 73, 73–75
Chivington, Jane, 15–16
Chivington, John Milton, xiv, 11, 17,
  22–23, 25; background of, 15–20;
  Black Kettle's camp approached by,
  123; Civil War and, 19; community as
  respecting and fearing, 16;
  controversial and condemned life of,
  98–102; Custer compared to, 60;
  damning testimonies against, 44;
  Democrats as viewed by, 62; denial of
  atrocities at Sand Creek Massacre by,
  46; as disagreeing with Whipple's
  article, 72; disgraced name and death
  of, xv, 113–114; divorce of Sarah and,
  73; Dog Soldiers as wanting answers
  from, 46; editorial staff positions, 73;
  end of military service for volunteers
  and, 40, 72; hero's treatment of, 40,
  111; knowledge of Sand Creek band as
  peaceful, 111; lawsuits involvement of,
  113; as leader in Methodist Episcopal
  Church, 16; life after Sand Creek
  Massacre of, 60–62; marriage and
  abuse to third wife Isabella, 72, 73,
  73–75; marriage to Rollason, 16;
  marriage to son's widow Sarah, 72;

ABOUT THE AUTHORS

Chris Enss is a *New York Times* best-selling author, scriptwriter, and comedienne who has written for television and film and performed on cruise ships and on stage. She has worked with award-winning musicians, writers, directors, and producers, and as a screenwriter for Tricor Entertainment, but her passion is for telling the stories of the men and women who shaped the history and mythology of the American West. Some of the most famous names in history, not to mention film and popular culture, populate her books. She reveals the stories behind the many romances of William "Buffalo Bill" Cody, who moved on from his career as a scout on the plains to bring the enormously successful performance spectacle of Buffalo Bill's Wild West to audiences throughout the United States and Europe between 1883 and 1916. And she tells the stories of the many talented and daring women who performed alongside men in the Wild West shows, changing forever the way the world thought about women through the demonstration of their skills.

Chris brings her sensitive eye and respect for their work to her stories of more contemporary American entertainers as well. Her books reveal the lives of John Wayne, Roy Rogers, and Dale Evans, bringing to light stories gleaned from family interviews and archives. The most famous American couple of the nineteenth century, General George Armstrong Custer and Elizabeth Bacon Custer, draws her scrutiny as well. Her book *None Wounded, None Missing, All Dead* (published by Globe Pequot) reveals the personality of the fiery, lively Libbie and her lifelong effort to burnish her husband's reputation. In other books, Chris takes readers along the trail with the Intrepid Posse as their horses thunder after the murderer of Dodge City dance hall favorite Dora Hand, and she turns her attention to the famous Sam Sixkiller, legendary Cherokee sheriff. But perhaps most extraordinary are the stories of the ordinary men and women who shaped American history when they came west as schoolmarms, gold miners, madams, and mail-order brides.

Howard Kazanjian is an author and award-winning producer and entertainment executive who has been producing feature films and television programs for more than twenty-five years. While vice president of production for Lucasfilm Ltd., he produced two of the highest-grossing films of all time: *Raiders of the Lost Ark* and *Star Wars: Return of the Jedi*. He also managed production of another top-ten box office hit, *The Empire Strikes Back*. Some of his other notable credits include *The Rookies*, *Demolition Man*, and the two-hour pilot and first season of *JAG*.

CPSIA information can be obtained
at www.ICGtesting.com
Printed in the USA
LVHW100518161222
735352LV00002B/26